Hillbilly Cornbread

Nancy Inman

Print information available on the last page

Rev. date: 02/15/2019

To order additional copies of this book, contact:
Xlibris
1-888-795-4274
www.Xlibris.com
Orders@Xlibris.com

Hillbilly Cornbread

Understanding what a HillBilly really is. The things that I learned in my Grandma's kitchen, a little bit about cooking and a whole lot about life!

NANCY INMAN

"Hillbilly Cornbread" is a "Southern" book with a perspective of how I view the world that we live in and my ideas along with both of my Grandmother's insight on how to manage your way through it all. There is also a little history that my family has "privy" to about our "Neck of the Woods". There is some history about some very influential people who lived and died in these parts. They made sure that their kinfolks could be guaranteed a place to live in a peaceful and quiet land in this part of God's country to live out their days on this Earth. There is something for everyone in this book so enjoy, Y'all!

The Definition of Hillbilly:

Hillbilly hil-bil-ly / 'hil bile' /

An unsophisticated country person.

(1.)   Associated with the remote regions of the Appalachians.

(2.)   Old fashioned term to describe an unsophisticated individual.

A Hillbilly is a person who lives in a rural and remote area in the South. Most often in the Appalachian mountains or sometimes Ozark mountains.

Therefore, he is isolated and somewhat out of touch with modern day culture.

The stereotype of a Hillbilly;

(1.)   Usually, he is a white Southerner.

(2.)   He wears worn out hats and smokes a pipe that he made from an ear of corn.

(3.)   He makes his own moonshine.

(4.)   His teeth are bad.

(5.)   He has a lack of knowledge or education.

(6.)   He has long hair and a long beard.

(7.)   He plays a banjo or a fiddle.

(8.)   He owns a shot gun and hunts his own food with it.

(9.)   His clothes are worn and tattered.

(10.)   He is happy and content with what he has.

Hillbillies are Southern mountain folk who do not necessarily fit the description of the stereotype of a hillbilly listed above. They are however;

(1.)   Hunters, farmers and artisans.

(2.)   They do hunt for their food and farm their land.

(3.)   They don't live in the swamps or the bayous or the Southern lowlands.

(4.)   They do come from the hollers and the hills.

(5.)   Even though they are a little rough around the edges, hillbillies are usually good natured, friendly, honest and forthright people.

(6.)   They may have a lack of education and a lack of knowledge of more modern culture but, they make up for it with their individualistic and charming, folksy ways.

(7.)   They are not rednecks.

(8.)   Hillbillies are fun loving and just all around sweet people.

(9.)   They are musically inclined and are very talented musicians in their own way.

(10.)   He makes do with what he has.

The Definition of Cornbread:

Cornbread or corn bread (korn'bred')

Bread made from cornmeal.

Noun/Cornbread-bread made primarily of cornmeal.

Quick bread-breads made with a leavening agent that permits immediate baking.

Corn cake-baked in a pan or a griddle. (Southern and Midland)

Cornpone-pone-Cornbread often made without milk or eggs and baked or fried (Southern)

Hushpuppy, hushpuppy-deep fried cornbread ball (Southern)

Johnnycake, journey cake-Cornbread usually cooked pancake style on a griddle. (Chiefly New England)

Batterbread, Spoonbread-Soft bread made of cornmeal and sometimes made with hominy, must be served with a spoon (Chiefly Southern).

The Definition of Hushpuppy:

A small, round or slightly oblong cake made of cornmeal and fried in deep fat. (They were made as a snack for the dogs to quiet them down while a meal was being prepared to be eaten).

Origion 1918-20

Noun (Chiefly Southern U.S.)

A small, unsweetened cake or ball of cornmeal dough fried in deep fat.

Deep-fried cornbread ball (Southern)

Chapter One

We going to make some real good cornbread y'all. But, first let's talk in the kitchen. You can learn a lot in a kitchen. You can learn how to cook and a little bit about life. In my case it was more about life than cookin'. I was taught my first cooking lessons and a lot about life in my Grandma Mollie's kitchen.

My Grandma Mollie had a two-bedroom house down in "Goose Holler" in Morristown. Morristown is in East Tennessee, the birthplace of Davy Crokett. Davy Crokett was a frontiersman from these parts who fought and died with the likes of James "Jim" Bowie and William Barret Travis.

Grandma's little 'ole house with it's tin roof and it's wooden swing on the front porch was a special place. Sometimes, when it would rain the family would all gather on the front porch and enjoy the raindrops beating hard on the tin roof in awe. A few times there would be too many of us children sitting on that old porch swing until we would break it out of the ceiling. But, when we would all fall down then we would all get back up and wipe ourselves off and have a good laugh.

"That's good advice for all that ails you!"

I remember her kitchen vividly. A table and chairs, an old china cabinet with no china in it and some other hutches and cabinets which she displayed family pictures and bric a brac on. She had no modern day appliances in her kitchen. She used an old washing machine with rollers on it to do her laundry which she kept hidden in the kitchen corner. Well, I found it one day and just about lost a hand and an arm in those rollers once, once was enough!

In Grandma Mollie's kitchen there was always someone passing through it. Some were relatives and some were family friends and some were people that I've never seen before. She sure was popular! People that weren't even related to her called her "Aunt Mollie". Maybe, because she seemed so interested in them and what they had to say. She made everyone feel special. Grandma Mollie was an empathetic listner.

She had a lot of grandchildren and made each of us feel special. There was Helen who had three children, Jenna Lee had three, Jack had his seven, Jerry had three, Dad (Bill) had us four, Jim had two and Anna Mae had three. Well, do the math. That's twenty-five grandkids in and out of her little 'ole house.

It was like Grand"ma" Central Station! "If a child is given the right enviroment and encouragement, he or she can grow and expand in many interesting ways."

Grandma Mollie's kitchen was always clean. If she wasn't cleaning it herself then it would be my female cousins and me or an aunt or two with a broom and a mop in hand, Grandma always said to devote yourself to doing the dirty work. She said that you'll be better off for it in the long run. If you keep doing the easy work, you'll never get a chance to improve.

"The benefits to doing what others don't want to do will be numerous and vast for you."

"Team-work makes the dream work!"

You gain something from being around people who fascinate you. Articulate what you recieve from those fascinating people. Such as laughter, learning about different interests or cultures and enjoyment of life together.

What amazes me the most about Grandma Mollie's kitchen is that there was always something prepared to eat for everyone. And with her modest home and her modest income she sure did feed a lot of mouths. Anyone who came to visit or to sit for a spell with Grandma Mollie was always offered something to drink or to eat. That's something that I learned from her and have taught my children to do also. It's the Southern way of proper manners.

My biggest memory of her kitchen was that it always seemed to smell of cornbread. Grandma Mollie lived on cornbread! When family or guest would come by to visit which was most every day, they would start in the living room and somehow they all made their way into Grandma Mollie's kitchen. They were smelling that cornbread. The family and friends and some of those people that I have never seen before sittin' at Grandma Mollie's kitchen table. I now think back and what I was really smelling was love.

Grandma Mollie was born November 10th, 1899 and lived to be ninety-two. She was a tall attractive woman with beautiful black hair. I watched her hair get grayer and grayer as she got shorter and shorter. But, she was still beautiful to me. The kind of beauty that gets better with age as they say.

She did like her occasional cigarette and she liked her Bruton's snuff too. She always had her spittoon sitting by her favorite chair in the living room. Sometimes, I would volunteer to run down to the corner store to purchase her Bruton's snuff just so I could be rewarded with a gumball or a five-cent soda pop. Or, sometimes I would get myself a moon pie, now that's Southern. Those were the days!

Grandma Mollie raised seven children by herself after my Grandfather Ralph died at an early age. He had come home one day and sat down to eat his supper that Grandma Mollie had prepared for him. Grandma Mollie had made him steak and bisquets with gravy. He started nibbling on some cut green peppers that she had laid out for him and while she was washing dishes he went to lay down. She heard him making some unusual noises while he was sleeping so she woke him up. He said that his feet were cold so Grandma Mollie washed his feet for him. The next day they sent for the doctor and he told him to go and lay down and my Grandfather Ralph never woke up. That was October 25, 1941.

That's a pretty tough situation for a woman of that time. With seven children and a few adopted children that she and Ralph took care of. But, Grandma Mollie persevered in spite of difficult times. Now, that's a strong woman.

I've heard a lot of stories about my Grandfather Ralph. He was tall, slender and had dark hair and dark eyes. I was told that his descendants had come over from England on a ship and that he had worked on the railroads in North Carolina. Working on the railroads and in the coal mines was a way of life in these parts back then.

So, it was all about Grandma Mollie. She never re-married, I guess she could have but, her life seemed to be filled with her family and friends. The family loved, admired and respected that woman.

She didn't have time to date for goodness sake. She worked at the laundry until she was seventy years old. She kept some of us grandkids until she decided that she was too old to work anymore. Then babysitting was her only job. And I'm glad that she was my babysitter because I have learned most everything I know from Grandma Mollie.

She said that hard work and frugal eating kept her alive. She said that she would eat cornbread and turnip greens and that she ate small amounts through out the day along with either steak or pork chops as long as her family was fed.

Grandma Mollie took care of all the grandchildren while the parents went off to their jobs. The little 'ole lady who lived in a shoe?

"We have a lot to learn from children, to be laughing and happy for no particular reason."

With all of those children running around laughing and playing at her house was truly mystical. With it's yellow cherry trees, mulberry trees and that huge black walnut tree swaying in the wind. The aroma of honeysuckle was abundant in her back yard. That sweet intoxicating smell would put a smile on your face. Beautiful Monarch butterflies would flutter all around her little old house.

We even had a Palomino mare, named "Lady". My Dad had bought her especially for me. She would ride us all along Grandma Mollie's back yard. We each took turns riding her and trying not to get hit by a falling walnut from that old walnut tree swaying in the wind!

When I was about nine years old I used to play by those big old trees in her back yard and I actually dug up out of the ground a silver spoon with my name, Nancy etched on it. Talk about mystical! You've heard the expression, "Born with a silver spoon in your mouth". Well, I had to dig my silver spoon up right out of Grandma Mollie's back yard!

When we slept over at Grandma Mollie's house she would pile tons of blankets on us to keep us warm in the winter time. If I didn't get a leg out from beneath all of those blankets I thought that I would surely die from all of those hand-made quilts on top of me!

Sometimes when my brothers and I would spend the night along with some of our cousins and after Grandma had fed us our supper, we would all gather in the living room to watch a movie on the television. But, you had to call your chair to get the best seat. Grandma had her recliner right there by her spit-toon and we would get what we got.

Growing up in those days, in the 1960's, we watched a lot of Doris Day movies along with Bob Hope and Jerry Lewis. They kept us all laughing back then. But, I liked the more mysterious movies like; "To Kill a Mockingbird". Gregory Peck's character, Atticus Finch was idealistic, strong and fair. Qualities that I admire in a father figure.

When "Gone with the Wind" played at the only movie theater in town my brothers, cousins and I trecked the five miles on foot to go and see it. We were given the money to pay for our tickets and to get ourselves a snack. I always opted for a very "large" sour pickle for my snack.

I was mesmerized by Vivian Leigh who played "Scarlet O'Hara". What made her more beautiful and interesting to me was the way that she cocked her one eye-brow everytime that she was up to something and she did that a lot!

Now that I am a lot older and a lot wiser I realize what Scarlett O'Hara mean't when she had to keep returning to her home which her family called, "Tara". I always feel better when I return home no matter how long that I have been away.

They named a street in Morristown after my Great-Grandfather John Alexander called, "Inman" street. "Inman" street was located a few streets over from Grandma Mollie and Ralph's house down in that holler and near "Inman Bend". Great-Grandfather John Alexander had a bunch of boys who helped work on that old muddy road with him. And after they had put tar on it to complete it the foreman who was put in charge of constructing the road told him "Well, seeing that you and all your bunch of boys mainly built this road, I guess that we should call it "Inman" street." I've been on that road through out my life and what a fine road it is!

So, I guess that Great-Grandfather John Alexander was well admired and respected also. I wish that I could of met him. I have often thought of my Great-Grandfather John and my Grandfather Ralph. I still feel their connection to our family. I believe that they must of had "Big" personalities. Where some personalities persist and others are forgotten, theirs lives on strong in the "Inman" family clan.

Grandma Mollie shared that holler with some very nice people. I remember some of the black folks who also lived down in that sweet, old holler would always smile and wave and say "Hello and how are you doing today Ms. Inman?" when they would pass by her house. They were always respectful to my Grandma and all of her family. As we were taught to be respectful back.

"Children learn by example. So, mind your manners!"

Grandma Mollie never drove a car and she didn't have to. Her children took care of her daily needs for her. They took her anywhere that she wanted to go. She went on family vacations with each of her children. Once, we took her to visit her son, Jack and his family in California. He had moved out West to help send our astronauts into space. He was in communications and helped us to stay in contact with our astronauts. She had taken several trips out to California and a few times she actually went by traveling in an airplane!

I remember our trip in the summer of 1970. After losing my suit-case from the top of our car somewhere near Las Vegas, Nevada, Mom and Dad decided to do a little gambling at the "Horseshoe" casino. Grandma Mollie did a little gambling too while she was keeping an "eye" on us kids running in and out of the casino.

"You've got to watch out for those 'Hillbillies.'"

We finally made it to Salinas, California to visit with Jack and Imo and their seven children. And we ate their artichokes that they grew in their back yard. Well, after they showed us how to eat them! So, I guess that I've got "Hillbilly" cousins all up and down the coast of California now.

We took Grandma Mollie to visit Disneyland and we took her to a West coast beach for the day and she enjoyed every minute of it! We also took her to the San Diego zoo where I watched the monkeys throw poop on my brothers, Mike and David. You've got to love the monkeys!

"We can all be ordinary people doing extraordinary things or extraordinary people doing ordinary things."

Family and friends used to send Grandma Mollie things too. Once, I opened up her lil' 'ole refrigerator and found some caviar and champagne. She let me taste the caviar but, not the champagne. Now I know why I have a hankerin' for caviar!

Grandma Mollie lived a full and exciting life for a little 'ole "Hillbilly". In her last will and testament she said that before she died that she would love to go back to California and to meet some of her great-grandchildren that she had never seen before. She wanted to be able to attend church again. But, most especially she wanted all of her family to live a good Christian life. Grandma Mollie was born to be a mother figure and a nurturer which involves faith, hope and trust.

"It is necessary to nurture the seedlings carefully in order to bring them to a healthy fruition. And so it is with children or relationships. They need firm foundations from which to grow strong and powerful."

Grandma Mollie had a unique sophistication about her. She was the epitome of wordly and wise. She taught us many things that we didn't even know that we were being taught. But, the biggest lesson she taught us was; Keep your humor and you'll find your way.

"God made us but, our ancestors had a hand in it."

Mollie Edith Inman 1899-1992

Silver Spoon with "Nancy" etched on it.

Chapter Two

I guess some people just get darn lucky because not only was I blessed with Grandma Mollie's kitchen to learn all of those wonderful things and to socialize with all of those wonderful people, I also learned a whole lot of other stuff from my Grandma Kat's kitchen. Grandma Kat is on my mother's side of the family.

She was called "Kat" which is short for Katheleen. Grandma Kat was a beautiful tall red-head from Irish descent. My sister, Carol Ann told me once that she took Grandma Kat to one of her family reunions and that she had never seen so many red-heads in one place!

When my brothers and I would spend the night with Grandma and Grandpa Talley we got a little taste of how farmers truly lived. This country was built by people just like them. If they didn't grow what they needed on their own farm land then other neighboring farmers would be happy to sell you some of their produce at a fair price.

Sometimes, I would take a ride with Momma up through the countryside to purchase a bushel of apples or peaches from someone's orchard. Most of the time you had to pick them yourself, though. My Momma, Betty Jo said that she and her sister, Willi Ann and brother, Darrell would gather up and sell chicken eggs to make a little extra money. So, support your local farmers!

Grandma and Grandpa had a well on their property to get their water supply from. I hated that smell of sulfur from the well water. I didn't look forward to a bath after a day of playing on their farm and out in the pastures. Nor did my brothers, Mike and David. And of course when they put us to bed at night then came all of those hand-made quilts on top of us to keep us warm and as usual I had to get a leg out or I would surely die!

Grandma Kat was musically talented. She played the guitar and the harmonica very well. She and her father, Howard Calfee and her two sisters, Polly and Carrie would get together and play a combination of Gospel and Bluegrass. That's called "Hillbilly" music where I come from. Her sister, Polly played the guitar also and her Father played the fiddle, (our version of the violin).

The girls were also in a quartet back then. They sang all up and down those hollers and hills. They didn't have lessons to learn how to play those instruments back then. They taught themselves how to play, "by ear". So, the whole family was musically talented whether they sang or played an instrument. They were doing what came naturally.

Some of that talent trickled down our family tree. My sister, Carol Ann played the piano and she had no lessons either. She was so good at it that she played the piano at our church. Church people call that a "calling". My brother, Mike and I however; took lessons for five years. We learned something but, our piano teachers kept dying on us. So, every year we would have to start all over! We kept trying until one old piano teacher would hit us on our fingers with a ruler when we would mess up and that was enough for us. That's when we took up sports!

None of that beautiful talent trickled down to my brothers and I. That's unfortunate because to watch someone play an instrument of any kind and to play it well is a blessing. "That old time mountain music still echoes through those hollers and hills."

I'll have to say, in my opinion, I think that Grandma Kat is the best cook that I have ever known. Everything that she cooked was from scratch. Her cakes were phenominal. My favorite was her infamous three layered apple stack cake. She picked those apples herself.

My brother, Mike and I share our birth date in December. Grandma Kat would bake us the tallest coconut cake that we had ever seen. No, she didn't grow the coconuts! When it would start snowing outside then we knew that we were getting that tall, coconut cake. We also got a new pair of crocheted house-shoes to go along with our tall, coconut cake that we looked forward to each and every birthday. "Try and appreciate the little things in life and remember that lost time does not return."

Grandma Kat is the one who taught me about a "seasoned" skillet. I'm still using the seasoned skillet that she seasoned especially for me to bake my cornbreads in. And boy, have I made a lot of them.

My Grandma Kat and Grandpa Homer lived in the country near Newport, Tennessee just below Gatlinburg. Those rolling hills unravel a string of farm lands, homesteads and the communties that stich them together. There are a lot of us Inman and Talley clans running around that "Neck of the Woods".

There is a place called "Inman Bend" which was not too far from Grandpa and Grandma Talley's farm and there is also a place a hop and a skip away from their farm called "Talley Hollow". "Talley

Hollow" was made up mostly from my Grandpa Talley's family. He was the eldest of eight boys who scattered all around those hills. Those "Hillbillies" are what we would call a "close-knit" family.

"Put down roots. There is a need for traditions and the passing down of benefits, whether material, emotional or purely genetic from one generation to the next."

Grandpa and Grandma Talley raised tobacco and a large garden on their farmland. So, they were self-sufficient. Grandma Kat canned her fruits and vegetables that she grew herself and I guess anything else that you can think of to put in a jar. She even canned sausage and pigs feet, eew! "Roll up your sleeves and dirty your hands with real life experience."

Shoot, they even made their own ice-cream. We didn't make that in the kitchen however; the whole family would gather outside by the picnic tables and participate in churning the cream, sugar, fruit and the main ingredient "love" until we all enjoyed a nice bowl of Grandma Kat's home-made ice-cream. I think that my favorite kind was strawberry.

My brothers and I sure did have a good time picking those strawberries because it gave us a chance to play in the fields, hither and yon. We would run and play and observe the cows and the horses and not to forget the 'ole bull that we tried to agitate. I believe that my brother, Mike actually rode that 'ole stinkin' bull. He and my brother, David were very adventurous!

"You have bravery, vitality and honesty within you so make every venture in your life exciting."

We didn't just pick strawberries on their farm. We picked grapes and blackberries too. When we would return back to Grandma Kat's kitchen with our basket full of blackberries our purple hands and our purple faces would give us away from have eaten our share!

I remember seeing my Grandpa's tobacco hanging up in his barn after he had harvested it. He was a tobacconist, (a dealer in tobacco). The ironic part is that he never smoked tobacco himself.

Grandpa Talley taught us many things. He worked hard and served his church and family. He showed us strength. Which indicates personal courage and self-discipline. Self-discipline and restraint are required if any goal is to be met. Without effort and endurance, nothing worthwhile can be accomplished.

"Thank you, Grandpa Talley."

Everything was a miracle and a wonder to us kids when we would visit their farm and Grandma

Kat's kitchen. You know that we could all learn a lot from folks just like them. And who knows, the way that this world is heading we may all have to. Don't underestimate surviving, it's harder than it looks. I know that we can't all live on a farm but, just by using what we need and not being wasteful could help turn this spinning world that we all live in around.

Part of the way that you pass down your legacy is to teach the ones that you love to do something that you know how to do. So, Grandma showed us girls how to cook, can food, sew and to crochet (needle-point). Grandpa Talley was a great carpenter as well. He showed the men in the family their way around a hammer.

Sometimes we fear that we won't be able to surpass what we've already accomplished. But, Grandma and Grandpa Talley taught us to stand tall, reach high, dream big and above all to believe in yourself.

Grandma Kat and Grandpa Homer were just good people. Their priorities in life were God first, family and working hard. Everything else came after that. They taught us that there are sufficient inner resources that may be drawn upon when life is at it's most demanding.

"Dig deep within yourself because there is always a hill to climb."

Self discipline and control are necessary in order to be able to carry on when life feels like a ton of bricks resting on your shoulders. Our methods for making choices may not always sit well with others. Try and make good choices that benefit you rather than making choices from just what you may desire. Always consider the consequences of your choices. Remember Adam and Eve had to live with their decision to eat the apple.

Take responsibility for your life's path rather than blaming fate for things that you don't like. It is a powerful course to take, though.

"Take responsibility for your own life."

Try to make memories in your life with your loved ones. Tranquility around you will eventually create tranquility inside you. So, ride the wave to happiness!

Now when you sit down at your kitchen tables with your families to eat your supper let's all try and remember to say Grace over what the Good Lord has given us and to thank the hands who helped to prepare it.

"Goals are achieved or realized through consistent hard work and rigorous attention to detail. Also, listen to your parents even though you may sometimes think that their rules and advice are arbitrary and/or unfair because they do know best."

Katheleen Calfee-Talley

Grandma Kat with Grandpa Homer and Betty Jo Talley

Great-Grandfather Howard Calfee, Grandma Kat and her cousin.

Chapter Three

I was raised in East Tennessee down by Cherokee lake in Talbott, which is forty-five miles to Gatlinburg up in the Smokey mountains and forty miles to Knoxville. The people around there really know their way around a kitchen. Making home-made bisquets and cornbread and all the fixins' that go with it. Usually, they get them right out of their own vegetable gardens.

My momma, Betty Jo has the best recipe for hushpuppies that you're ever gonna taste. Living down by Cherokee lake you've got to have a "fish fry". Well, we had a few "fish fries" at our house. You get the family together and invite some friends over. Hopefully, someone with a guitar or a banjo so that you can enjoy some music while you are eatin' some of the best fish and hushpuppies and the fixins' that you can sink your teeth into.

My dad, Bill had his trot line set up every summer and we were hooked-up with the fish. The best catfish, crappi, rainbow trout and bass fishing ever. Down South they say; "Reel in something big or at least a big story". I've reeled in a few and had a "Big" story or two myself!

Mom's recipe for the hushpuppies is basically the same for the cornbread with a few "extra" ingredients. Yeah, I'm going to give y'all the recipe from her, with her blessing. Her hushpuppies were so good and infamous that a local seafood restaurant tried to buy the recipe from her. No, she didn't sell it. She always said that one day she would have her own restaurant to sell them at. She did for awhile but, you know how in life that nothing last forever. Well, except maybe her hushpuppy recipe!

I sure did enjoy living down by Cherokee lake. My parents, Bill and Betty Jo bought a house in "Green Acres". It was a beautiful two-story, gray brick colonial home on two acres of land. With it's ivy growing on the front of the house and the dainty wrought iron chairs on the front porch and it's long driveway with horse jockey statues along side beautiful schrubbery brought out it's Southern charm.

It had a huge oak tree in the front yard that would look dead in the winter time but, would come back to life in the spring time. I spent a lot of time in that big 'ole tree. Once you climbed it and got up there high enough, well you might as well spend some time in it!

I would do a lot of my serious thinking and a little spying up in that big old tree. I guess you could say that I was scopin' out the perimeter. Y'all know how young girls need a quiet place to contemplate their futures.

Back in the seventies I don't think that we locked our doors that often, we didn't have to back then. The world seemed to be a lot more peaceful and less hectic. In the summer evenings we would leave the windows open to get the cool breeze blowing in along with the sound of crickets chirping, toads croaking and the occasional smell of a skunk. I did not like that part of it but, the other stuff would put you to sleep like a baby. Now, that's Southern charm.

Momma was about as good a cook as Grandma Kat was. She paid attention to her lessons in the kitchen. It didn't take her anytime at all to whip up a cornbread and the fixins' to go with it in her kitchen.

Now, we have "Big" breakfasts' down South. We don't do "Brunch". We could have a lunch if your still hungry after your "Big" breakfast but, I doubt it. We have dinner around two-ish, especially on Sunday after church. Supper is what y'all call dinner. We eat supper if your still hungry after dinner and that is served in the evening. Are you confused?

Down South we don't just serve cornbread with our main meals. Sometimes, we serve it as our dessert too. I used to watch my Momma cut a slice of cornbread and crumble it up in a glass of milk or sometimes buttermilk. Try it sometime, it's not too bad.

My dad, Bill on the other hand was one of the best characters that I have ever had the pleasure of knowing. And I am happy and proud to have been his daughter. They say when he was a little boy that he didn't talk until he was five years old. And one day out of the blue he said; "I want a mayonaise sandwhich". Well, then they couldn't shut him up. His family and friends called him, "Motor Mouth". And all of his hunting buddies called him, "Beaver Jaws", lovingly of course. I am my Father's daughter. The apple didn't fall to far from the tree as they say.

"A busy boy is a good boy", and Bill stayed busy. He worked at a textile plant as an air-condition technician until he retired after thirty-two years of service. He was also a retired sergeant in the U.S. army and did summer camps at Fort Bragg, North Carolina. Along with being in the Color Guard, he also volunteered for the Morristown, Tennessee Resque Squad for twenty-eight years. If that didn't keep him busy enough, he was a professional bowler, avid hunter, fisherman and played on a softball league.

He was once scouted for the Cleaveland Indians baseball team. They chose him to take up North to join their team but, Dad hurt his arm and they had to take his buddy instead. I remember once he and Mom took us to Ohio to see his friend in action and we kids were rewarded with an autographed baseball from the whole team!

He was always teaching us kids how to do something. He showed us all about guns and gun saftey, of course. He taught my brothers how to hunt. They would track and shoot deer or sometimes use a bow and arrows for their hunting expeditions. They would also frog gig or catch snapping turtles for Mom to fry up. And when Mom would fry the frog legs, we kids would have to watch her so that we could see them "jumping" in the frying pan.

Some people heard about that turtle hunting and wanted to film a documentary about it. So, they went with my Dad and brothers and some of my Dad's "Hillbilly" cousins on a turtle hunting expedition. Those crazy men would put their hands in that muddy water and pull those snapping turtles up by their tails. They couldn't make the documentary about it however; because they didn't know that there would be that much damn cussin' going on!

Cherokee lake is a beautiful sight to see. The Tennessee Valley Authority keeps the state and the lakes looking good. If you ever want to move South, you may want to come and look my "Neck of the Woods" over for an authentic Tennessee experience. I bet that you will not want to ever go back to wherever you are from.

My family thoroughly enjoyed living on Cherokee lake. If we were not camping around it, fishing in it, riding motorcycles around it, houseboating on it or pontoon boating all around it well, we were "skinny dipping" in it!

Some days we would watch the deer swimming their herd across the lake or we would see them roaming in the fields off the beaten path. We used to feed the deer dried corn across from our property to keep them out of our vegetable garden and from eating our corn that we grew. Some of our neighbors would put a salt lick on their trees to get the deer onto their property so they could shoot them out of season. That's not fair!

My brother, Mike learned a big lesson. He and his friend once shot a deer out of season and the

Wild Life and Game officer who found out about it put them both in Wild Life school to teach them all about the rules and regulations of hunting deer. He never did that again!

Hunting and fishing is and always will be a way of life wherever you are from. If you respect what you are hunting or fishing for than there should be no problem. We eat what we kill. We as hunters are taught to respect all life and to be responsible hunters.

My Dad was a responsible hunter and always played by the rules. He had a few of his deer heads mounted on the den walls and the freezer full of deer meat. Mom would marinate the roast of the deer meat in vinager and water to get rid of the game taste but, not the deer chops or the deer ground meat. It was a flavor thing.

Dad was what you would call a "Man's Man". The kind of man that other men wanted to hunt with, fish with or have on their sports team. He was just that good and fun to be around.

Now, Dad could find something to eat out in those woods and know how to cook it but, he sure couldn't find anything in our kitchen and cook it!

He probably would have starved to death if it wasn't for Mom. Mom went to Myrtle Beach, South Carolina once with her girlfriends and left Dad at home with us kids. We all just about starved to death that week!

"Thank the Lord for those Southern women and their Southern kitchens!"

Dad was also very patriotic. Wherever we went if the national anthem was being played or if the American flag was being raised or lowered he had his hand on his heart and a tear in his eye.

So, fly your flags high folks for this great country that we live in and put your hands over your hearts when you see it flying and swaying in the wind from the highest mountain tops and from sea to shining sea.

Snapping Turtle and Bullfrog

Chapter Four

I'm sure that someone in your family has a recipe that has been passed down from generation to generation. And I'm sure that those family members passed down a whole lot of love with their directions too. I hope that each time that you prepare those dishes that you remember like I do the memories and the love that was added to each dish because that is what makes them taste better.

Are you ready now for my cornbread recipe?

How about those hushpuppies?

Ok, I'll give them to you before we leave the kitchen.

Since I've never seasoned a black iron skillet before I had to call Grandma Kat. Oh, by the way, she is ninety-eight years old. I had to ask her for these directions on how to season your skillet. I hope that you'll appreciate it like I do and if you want to you can pass this down to your family and friends with love.

Grandma Kat says to season your skillet that all you have to do is get yourself a good size black iron skillet. Then wipe it down real good all over with vegetable oil. Turn your oven on to 500' degrees and bake your skillet for about twenty minutes. Repeat the process and you have just "seasoned" your skillet. Now, all you have to do after you bake each cornbread is to wipe the skillet out. Never wash it. Boy, the kitchen sure does smell good after baking a cornbread. You'll get a hankerin' for some.

I don't normally cook with directions. Usually, it's a little bit of this and a little bit of that. So, I went into the kitchen and got my measuring cups out especially for y'all.

When I was taught how to cook something in the kitchen it was usually by watching the women folk preparing their dishes. Ain't nobody using a cookbook. I never asked any of the ladies for a recipe book. Their women folk showed them how to cook. They taught us how to make "Hillbilly" cuisine, a style of their own. That's just the way it was. They also taught us the way to a man's heart is through his stomach. So, listen up ladies!

I do remember the ladies being beautiful and smart. Let's see: We had Jenna Lee, Jewel Dean, Betty Jo, Paula, Imo, Anna Mae, Willi Ann, Linda, Brenda and Carol Ann. Boy, if that doesn't sound like some Southern women then I don't know what does. Back then it was common for folks to have several names. I was named after my great-Grandmother, Nancy Alice Augusta Matilda White. Try that name on for size.

My favorite aunt was Jenna Lee. Maybe, because she spent a lot of time with my brothers and I. It really did seem like she was teaching us. She had books about almost everything you could think of at her house. Math books, philosophy books. Art, engineering and so many others.

She didn't go to college and probably would have but, she had to help out after her father died at an early age. Jenna Lee, being one of the eldest of Grandma Mollie's children helped raise those kids. And after each one would go off to school she would read and study their books. She would spend hours telling us stories and teaching us things. She even taught my brother, Mike how to crochet!

You don't have to get your education from a school house. Once she told me that it is necessary to accept all aspects of our nature, both dark and light. So, that our repressed fear can be released to give way to liberated, positive energy. If this isn't permitted, inhibitions and phobias can accumulate unconsiously, preventing healthy growth. That's some pretty good advice from a "Hillbilly".

And then there was Jewel Dean. I just loved looking at her. She was married to my Dad's older brother, Jerry. She came from Cherokee Indian descent and was just naturally beautiful. I still have some of the things that she gave me as a child. She once gave me a beautiful antique colonial pendant. I'll pass that pendant down to my Granddaughter and tell her all about her Great-aunt Jewel Dean one day.

My most fond memory of her was making outfits from leaves off a mulberry tree from Grandma Mollie's backyard. Her and my Mom peiced together those large leaves and made us kids clothes and hats. We all looked like little Peter Pans' running around the backyard with our little outfits she and Mom made for us. See, it doesn't cost anything to have a whole lot of fun, you just got to make it fun.

Now, Anna Mae was the aunt that was easy on the eyes. She had blond hair and big brown eyes. She was demour with her classic good looks. She is the epitome of a Southern lady. She, like all of the women in our family also knew her way around a kitchen. Anna Mae showed all of us girls how to make a mince pie. I havn't had a mince pie as good as that pie we made back when I was ten years old.

Brenda was married to Jenna Lee's eldest son. She really did try to entertain us kids. Sometimes, we would wake up at Grandma Mollie's house and underneath all of those handmade quilts we would find sparklers, silver dollars or candy that Brenda would sneak in and put them there for us to find. Heck, this woman even took us "Snipe" hunting!

She really set us kids up for our snipe hunting trip. She and some of my aunts sat all of us in Grandma Mollie's kitchen and told us that we were going to go snipe hunting. When we asked what a "Snipe" was she told us that we would know when we saw one. They told us to get our pots and spoons together so that we could beat on them to draw the snipes out of the bushes and the trees. They then drove us to a remote spot out by a field and let us all out. All of us kids running around the field beating our pots with our spoons and calling out, "here Snipe", "here Snipe", until we were exhausted. When we exclaimed that we couldn't catch a snipe all of the adults laughed out loud and told us probably because there was no such thing as a "Snipe"! Boy, did we feel foolish but, we had a great time learning that lesson.

"Life is for the living. So, live your life, enjoy your life until your life is at it's end."

When the family all got together at Grandma Mollie's house for occasions it seems as though her kitchen grew bigger. Each family brought dishes to put along side of Grandma's dishes of fried chicken, fried green tomatoes, mashed potatoes, corn on the cob, hand picked green beans, sweet potatoe casserole, bisquets and of course, cornbread just to name a few.

And when the occasion at her house was Christmas, not only was Grandma's kitchen full of wonderful food to eat there were Christmas gifts galore for everyone and especially, for Grandma. Her Christmas tree had so many gifts under it, I swear they took up the whole living room!

She always opted for a cedar tree for her Christmas tree. Then she would pin dollar bills on the bottom of the tree for my little cousins so that they could reach them. I don't know how Grandma Mollie managed it but, she always had me a box of store bought chocolate covered cherries under it. And to this day every time that I eat a chocolate covered cherry I think of her and her thoughtfulness. Now, that's Southern charm with charm to spare!

Coming from a large family I had a variety of characters to observe as a child. I'm pretty sure that I learned something from each of them. Anything from religion, politics and cooking to how in their opinions to catch the biggest fish. Some lessons were good and some were not so good.

I guess that's the thing about a lesson, some you learn the easy way and some you have to learn the hard way. When you get your lessons then you take them and manage them throughout your life. I hope y'all have a long life and I hope especially, that you are a good manager. Life is about letting go and moving forward so don't let anything have power over you. Those lessons that I learned in my Grandma's kitchens will remain with me forever.

Each story that you hear in your life will have a bit of learning inside for you, and the same goes for the stories that you'll tell. Telling stories is a way to absorb and process the beautiful world that we live in.

They say that you take all of what you learn in this life with you when you pass over. Heaven and Earth are both full of things that we don't fully understand. This life is a blink of an eye compared to our eternal life. We are here to learn lessons so, learn all of the good stuff that you can and try not to learn any foolishness!

"If your gonna be dumb then you gotta be tuff!"

"When our time is up, Rise up! The sky is never ending."

Nancy's Black Iron Skillet

Aunt Jewel's colonial pendant

Chapter Five

If you are inclined to do so you may want to take a trip to my "Neck of the Woods". Paying homage to other worlds is both respectful and enjoyable. Maybe, you don't belong there permanetly. But, you applaud and honor another person's way by participating in it. What a beautiful place Tennessee is. From the hollers to the mountains and from the lakes to the streams.

Those mountains are majestic. That's why they call them "The Great Smokey Mountains". The Cherokee Indians named the mountains "Shaconage" (Sha-co-na-ge), meaning the "Place of Blue Smoke".

I spent a lot of time in those mountains and them there hills. My family would vacation there every summer for weeks at a time. We would all go camping to enjoy hiking, fishing and touring the sites of the "Smokies".

You can smell mountain laurel which is indiginous to the area everywhere. It grows all over the mountain. And the air is so clean and pure that it is breath taking.

The Cherokee Indians have a reservation about thirty-five miles out of Gatlinburg, Tennessee in Cherokee, North Carolina. I remember my family taking us to an outside play there that the natives put on at dusk called; "Unto These Hills". It's a play about "The Trail of Tears". How the Cherokee, Musojee (Creek), Seminole, Chickasaw and Choctaw nations (Collectively referred to as the five civilized tribes) survived a horrible fate at the hands of white settlers on this American continent in order to secure their land from them.

At the beginning of the 1830's, nearly 150,000 Native Americans lived on millions of acres of land. The land was mostly in around Tennessee, Alabama, North Carolina, Georgia and Florida. The land that their ancestors had occupied and cultivated for many generations. But, by the end of the decade there were very few Natives remaining anywhere in the Southeastern United States.

While working on behalf of the white settlers who wanted to grow cotton on the Indians' land, the federal government forced them to leave their homelands and walk hundreds of miles to a specially designated "Indian Territory" across the Missippi River. This was a hard and sometimes deadly journey and know as "The Trail of Tears".

The Cherokee language for this event is called; Nu na da ul tsun yi. It means; "The place where they cried".

"The Trail of Tears" is a name given to the ethinic cleansing and forced relocation of Native Americans from Southeastern parts of the United States. Following the Indian Removal Act of 1830. Davy Crokett ("King of the Wild Frontier"), who was elected to the U.S. Congress vehemently opposed many of the policies of Andrew Jackson, most notably the "Indian Removal Act".

Davy Crokett had an idea about how things should be. And while in office his vision would drive a whole lot of people forward.

"Fairness and equality bring Harmony".

"Hoo-ray" for Davy Crokett!

Years ago I actually found some old Indian pottery on my property in Gatlinburg, Tennessee. Turns out that those old bowls were made by the Cherokee Indians. I am honored to have found them and they are priceless to me.

Just to think about how self-sufficient that they were to make their own bowls, clothing and everything else that they needed is of epic porportions.

This should inspire us to embody our own gifts and talents more fully. Self sufficiency is an attractive quality. Our society today takes these necessities for granted. Imagine for a moment if you had to make the bowl that you had to eat from. We could all learn something from these wonderful people.

My brothers, Mike and David and I used to find arrow heads that the Cherokee Indians made quiet often when we were growing up in East Tennessee. We still have some of them. We were impressed by their craftsmanship even as children.

You can tour some of the Cherokee Indian museums in the area and enjoy looking at their tools and crafts if you ever want to visit where I come from.

I would like to thank the American Indians for introducing the first settlers to this continent to corn. Without corn we wouldn't be eatin' any of these wonderful and tasty cornbreads!

The Great "Smokey" Mountains, Gatlinburg, TN.

Cherokee Indian Bowls

Cherokee Indian Arrowhead

Chapter Six

Mom and Dad liked to take us kids to Cade's Cove, which is located above Gatlinburg and just before you get to Cherokee, North Carolina. There you will find a motor-nature trail that you can drive along and tour the sites. You can stop at some of the old log homes and churches that are still there or you can walk around some of the old graveyards dating back to when us "Hillbillies" came to these parts.

"Hillbillies put down roots in those hollers and hills".

The sunshine glistens on the majestic waterfalls that you will pass by and again there's that aromic smell of mountain laurel. Groves of it bloom in their glory every where that you go. You can gaze upon the landscape of those beautiful "Blue Smoked" mountains stretching all the way to the horizon. You could be distracted from your main focus of enjoying the beautiful landscape but, it's more fun to wander off course.

Try to appreciate and nuture the beauty in the world around you. Your soul will be fortified by a little wild beauty. Mother Nature is both amazing and incredible. "Those who stopped to smell the roses will inspire those who stopped to plant the seeds."

You can stop by one of the many river streams and picnic on the river's bank like we used to do. There you can let the "whole world" go by as you skip rocks into those exquisite flowing waters rushing over moss covered creek rocks. It will overwhelm your senses with it's intoxicating ambiance.

Now, don't forget to bring your bathing suits and your inner-tubes so that you can mosey around in those gorgeous streams for awhile. The waters current will spend you around and around all the way down the river. I would always find myself a good "walking stick" to help guide my inner-tube through the water and over those slick rocks. Some of those rushing waters will take you further than you want to go. My little brother, David and I had to walk about a mile once to re-unite with our loved ones and then we wanted to do it again!

There are lots of wilderness trails to follow off the road up through the "Smokies". You can enjoy looking at the unique wild flowers or you may see some of the wild life such as the deer that roam all through those woods. We would visit all of those wonderful and interesting sites for most of the day until we were tired and then we would make our way back to our cozy campsites with Grandma Mollie in tow.

Sometimes we would make it back to our campsite to find out that a bear had beat us to it. Seems bears like cornbread too! We eventually had to start securing our food supply. My Dad would have to put some of our food in bags and tie it high in a nearby tree to keep them from it. Signs are posted all over the park to "Do Not" feed the bears. So, don't feed the bears, dummy!

If and when any of the Black bears would make it out of the woods and into the camping areas the Park Rangers would re-locate them to a higher area up in the mountains. But, it was still exciting to see one every now and then. Sometimes while riding up those mountain roads you could get a glimpse of a momma bear and her baby cubs following close behind.

We always had a camper and some of my aunts, uncles and cousins would have their campers adjacent to ours. And when there was a bear sited in the camping areas, the Park Rangers and everyone camping in the park would get a tin and something to beat it with. We would all walk the park pathways beating our tin lids and making lots of noise until we felt safe enough to finally crawl into our sleeping bags and go to sleep. Those Park Rangers and employees of the park are very hospitable people. Being friendly comes naturally to Tennesseans.

We would wake up the next morning to the smell of Mom cooking our breakfast and listening to the leaves rustling in the wind. And if it had rained the night before we would see the wild ferns that grow there with their morning dew dripping off their fronds after that Smokey Mountain rain. We would then gather up our fishing gear after eating our wonderful breakfast that Mom had made for us and head to our favorite spot down at the river's bank to enjoy our beautiful summer's day.

I loved going fishing in those mountain streams. We would have our fishing rods or our cane poles with us and put our corn or worms on our hooks and race to see who could catch the first "Rainbow" trout, which are abundant in those river streams. And boy, do they love corn!

If we could not catch anything then we would lay down our poles and take off our shoes to wade in the cold water to look for crawdads or anything else that was swimming around in that water to investigate or to play with. We all have the capacity to derive pleasure from the simple things in life no matter how young or old we are. Laughing is a worthy endeavor. Laughter is not only good for the soul, it is also catching. You laugh, I laugh, you cry, I cry. So, let's all laugh together. "To the good life, may it last forever."

Family camping in Smokey Mountains

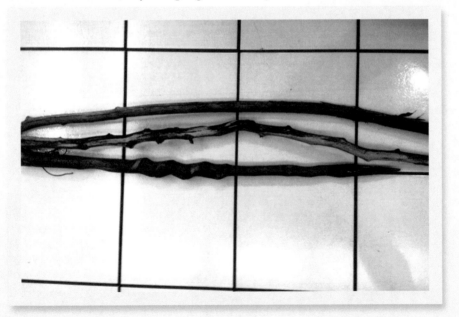

Some of my "Walking" sticks

Chapter Seven

"If you don't Stand up for something then you'll Fall for anything."

I'd like to tell you a story about a little situation called the Revolutionary War, y'all. About how North Carolina, South Carolina and Tennessee back country militia men or "Hillbillies" as we call them, took on Major Patrick Ferguson on Kings Mountain.

Around the end of the 1700's the British were focused on the Southern states. The British believed that the Southern colonies were largely Loyalist and, based on this assumption, built a military campaign to try to control the South. Major Ferguson, who headed up this military campaign sent a message down South threatening Southern Patriots with death if they did not submit to the Loyalist.

The Southern Patriots were mostly farmers, hunters and artisans who lived in the remote valleys, hollers and hills. They were rugged individuals of mostly Scots-Irish ancestry. They had little to do with the politics and events that were taking place up North. They were used to being independent and just minding their own business. Until, however; Major Ferguson made his threat against the Southerners. He must of thought that the world would bow down to his commands. So, then the Southerners were "Madder than a Hornet's nest."

"When times are taxing or testing then every bit of energy and might is needed to fend off challenges or to keep enemies at bay."

Some of the Southerners got together and formed a militia. They came together on horseback but, mostly on foot. The "Over-Mountain Men" as they were called came mostly from Tennessee, North Carolina and South Carolina. Some crossing the icey mountain foot paths that the Indians had used to join their forces together.

When Ferguson heard about this militia that was coming after him like "White on Rice", he tried to "Hightail" it back up North. He made it as far as Kings Mountain located in South Carolina by the North Carolina and Tennessee borders.

Now, those "Over-Mountain Men" who went after Ferguson fought "Indian style". Using the Indians techinque, they would make a surprise ambush with war hoops and yells and then they would retreat far back into the forest. This would lure Ferguson's soldiers into the woods where they would then overtake them. Major Ferguson called them barbarians and the dregs of mankind. What they really were was skilled woodsmen and hunters.

"Folks looking for trouble seem to find more than they're after."

Major Ferguson swore that he would take that mountain or he would die on that mountain. Well, he's buried on that mountain!

"I wouldn't underestimate those "Hillbillies" 'cause they might just out smart ya!"

"Failure is not an option. Never give up, never surrender!"

Later Cornwallis would surrender his British army to General Washington at Yorktown, Virginia and the Revolution was soon over.

"It takes courage, determination and perserverance to overcome rivals and to combat opponents."

One of my ancestors was part of the militia, "The Over-Mountain Men" that fought in the battle at Kings Mountain according to reliable sources. Abednego Inman who was one of three brothers who came over from York County, England. He went by the name of Bed Inman, (according to his signature of his last will and testament). Abednego was the youngest of the three Inman brothers. The eldest brother being Shadrach (1747-1830) and the next eldest Meshach (1748-1768). And then there was Abednego (1752-1831). According to the D.A.R. (Daughter's of the Revolution), his service was recorded in the Revolutionary war record. This service seems to have been established by the Patriot forces against the Loyalist forces. Acceptance of his service record by the Daughters of the American Revolution is found under National D.A.R. numbers; 144440, 13957, 16654, 16656 and 24409 and possibly others.

One of the groups that made up the "Over-Mountain Men" was led by John Sevier. Eventually, he became a politician here in these parts and was well respected. They even named a town after him called, Sevierville. Sevierville, Tennessee is located before you get to Pigeon Forge and Gatlinburg. They call it the "Foothills of the Smokies". There's a saying around this "Neck of the Woods", "Live Free or Die Hard".

John Sevier was one of America's first frontier statesmen. He was regarded as one of the best frontier leaders in American history.

He was nicknamed, "Nolichucky Jack". The Cherokee called him Tsan-usdi (Little John). A Cherokee warrior chief, Dragging Canoe named him.

Sevier's experience as a woodsman and his natural ability to lead was what aided him in crisis. In order to be a good leader in those days, you had to crawl alongside your men and lead them just as much as by example as you did by barking out orders.

"It's as important to finish strong as it is to start strong."

Now, I've given you a little history about what a "Hillbilly" really is and a little bit about what they are about. People with moral ethics and integrity. They are loyal and steadfast. If they have to impose their will it points to: The reconciliation of the opposites and the resolution of differing opinions. Harmony and alliance, always taking into both sides of any situation. Sometimes they must make difficult decisions but, they face those situations honestly and only then do they get through them.

Although ideas have been turned into action, and the groundwork has been done, there is still work to do. And even though there are many obstacles ahead a strong willed "Hillbilly" can overcome them. They make big sacrifices in order to bring about improvements. The essence of sacrifice is that it requires the voluntary surrender of one thing in order to improve the chances of getting something that you want more.

"Strength in the face of any adversity."

A "Hillbilly" is someone who is just and commited to causes he believes in, and is likely to be either a firm friend or an enemy to be reckoned with. They are people who take a restrained and reasonable course of action when necessary.

They are people who just want to live in their little neck of the woods and mind over their own. They want to live a quiet and peaceful existence in this part of God's country. And what a heavenly part of God's country it is.

They want to grow their own corn and eat their own cornbreads in peace and quiet. I hope that wherever you hail from that it is also heavenly and that you can find the same solace to live out your days.

"The time is right for a period of self-appraisal, which involves taking an honest look at yourself, your actions and your motivations."

In life you must choose your battles carefully, for some of them aren't worth fighting. And if and when you choose to fight you may know what you're up against, but do you know what you are in for? When you choose your battles then you have to have what it takes to see them through to the end.

"Real courage has some fear. Without fear is just foolish!"

So, strive y'all to contribute to a healthy, functional enviroment even though faced with largely disfuntional elements. And remember this my friends; If the inner animal urges within each man can be used in a positive way, great things can be achieved and/or accomplished.

If ignorance is the root to all evil, then it makes more sense to teach than to fight. Unfortuatley, not everyone is open to learning. We learn by example, so be a good teacher and in our live-time maybe we'll have some good students and all of this could change. You must teach from your own kitchens. Aunt Jenna Lee once told me that Shakespeare once said; "Love all, trust a few, do wrong to none."

"You can't change the direction of the wind but, you can adjust your sails."

"If you don't change something then nothing changes at all."

LAST WILL AND TESTAMENT OF ABEDNEGO INMAN

In the presence of thes witnes present I acknoleg this my last will and testament. This land I now live on I give to my three suns Shedrach Inman, Benjamin Inman and John Inman at my wifes decease.

My thre dayters Annes Cowan, Polly Bair and Peggy Harriet Wood the remaind of my estat after my lawfiil detes is payd. I do not alow enything to be desttrebuted in during my wifes netuel lifetime but what I leeve sole executors of this my last will and desire it to be recevd the sem. I do not alou the land to be sold or devded into eny smauler porcels but the executors to do what tha think is rite and gusth the entry includ as land. Witness my hand this twevth day May One thousand eight hundred and thirty.

witnes   s/Bed Inman
Nicholas Bragg

Mary her X mark Bragg

Archband T. McSpadden

State of Tennessee

Jefferson County March Sessions 1831

Chapter Eight

I have a place up in the "Smokies" that I spend with my family and some of my childhood friends. Yes, I still go fishing, hiking and inner-tubing along those ageless streams up and down those mountains. I also visit the sites each year and each visit is like the first time that we have ever met.

The excitement and the awe of it all will fill you up. Everytime that I see that mountain laurel and smell it's aroma is like we are old friends meeting again and again. It's like my senses have been deprived and I have to make up for lost time.

Those mountains and rivers define the landscape and lifestyle of East Tennessee. The peaks of those Southern mountain tops loom large over the Native American settlements and the vast flowing rivers nourish farmlands of old pioneer communties.

"That mountain culture still thrives."

And when I leave the mountains and head toward my old stompin' grounds, I'll head toward Cherokee lake. That's where I'll visit with Momma for a nice home cooked meal in her kitchen. She'll prepare me a nice baked cornbread and all the fixins' that go with it. And later after Momma's wonderful Southern dinner that she prepared especially for us, we'll all sit for a spell in her living room to catch up with the family and family matters.

Before I leave her house she'll have packaged me up some beautiful Tennessee tomatoes for my travels. And before I can get out the door I'll have my Tennessee tomatoes, some clothes, make-up and jewelry that she'd done went out and bought for me along with a few family heirlooms that she insist that I have before she dies!

Then I've got to find room in my car to squeeze everything she gave me in alongside of my luggage and all the creek rocks and walking sticks that I put there to take home with me. Of course, I have to take everything that she gave me and thank her kindly, because that's just good manners.

"Good manners is about kindness and respect."

Then we're off to go and see Grandma Kat. Grandma Kat will tell me all about her life when she grew up in those hollers and hills of East Tennessee. I love hearing each and everyone of her stories. But, she also teaches me other things such as; Life requires the virtues of patience, perserverance and tolerance. That's good advice that we should all heed. She's smarter than the average cat. She has lived to be ninety-eight and is still holding her own. I think that she knows something about something. Grandma Kat says; "Like looking for treasure find your blessings." And when you are grateful for each part of a blessing then blessings will keep coming."

I want to be able to pass these stories and words of wisdom from this wise woman and all the other strong Southern women in my family down to my grandchildren when they come to my kitchen to visit.

When I leave Tennessee and I leave my beautiful family and friends to come home, I'll look up into the dark sky and look to find a star. Seeing that big, bright star makes me think of what that shinning star really means. The star is an image of hope and promise. It indicates a sense of purpose, a goal to reach for and ambitions to aim towards. "Make ambitions come true on a practical and material level."

The sight of stars in the dark night sky are spiritually symbolic. They have always been associated with awe and mysterious powers. The star brings hope and belief that things will come right, even when they have been very difficult. The star represents the will to live and the optimism not to give up no matter how tough things may be. "You can't take a road or a route without first understanding what road your own now."

Take the time to make yourself comfortable and happy, because this is condusive to the best attitude. Your attitude will take you beyond the point that ability and motivation ever could.

We all share a quest for truth, beauty and love. You need to cultivate love in your heart. Love comes with both love and sorrow, both must be experienced. When you can't find the sunshine outside then know that there is sunshine within you.

"I will stand on my own."

Try to expand your understanding of the meaning of life. Try to search for the truth, philosophical or spiritual. Your intuition hasn't led you wrong yet, and it won't as long as you dare to follow it through to the end.

"While your ambition tries to push you forward, sometimes your intuition can hold you back."

It is then that you become aware that happiness is balanced by sadness and that makes sense. Every ending is a new beginning of a new story, y'all. One day at a time. So, the star is a welcome sight for sore eyes.

"Never complain, never explain. Smile, hide every trace of sadness. What's the use of crying? Just smile."

Chapter Nine

"If you can do a little bit, then do it. That little bit will turn out to be not only better than nothin' but, also what inspires and motivates other people to do more."

My Grandma Mollie and my Grandma Kat were both highly intelligent women. They both had something to share and to contribute to each family member. These ladies had a significant and profound impact on each of us.

They were both emotionally ambitious and filled with courage, which makes for the perfect teacher. And of course, their classrooms were their kitchens.

"To be an excellent teacher, you must communicate clearly."

I did learn this in their kitchens; If your life isn't everything that you had hoped for, try and find a hidden greatness in it. If you can find things to appreciate in your life and articulate that appreciation, well then you may come out a winner in this world afterall.

Those ladies were the "Queens" of their hearth. Their love is as strong as sunshine, which stretches and permeats around all that they love and care about. Their families and their personal lives were very important to them.

You must gain a sense of perspective in your own personal lives. Know what your priorities in life are and act on them accordingly. Make necessary and desirable changes in your life. Say goodbye to an old way of life if it isn't productive. Without death there is no new life only stagnation.

"Life is like a gem, don't let life rub you the wrong way."

They were wise women. Maturity and patience can be peaceful, the thrust of youth is no longer important. Accept rather than fight the passage of time because the rewards are patience, tolerance and serenity. That's something to look forward to ladies as we all grow to become older women.

"Ladies, you'll need a wishbone, a funny bone and a back bone to get you through life."

Another lesson that they taught us is how important learning our geneology is. Know "where" you come from and "who" you come from to know "who" you are. There are many ways to explore your geneology or family tree. You can go through records at the library, courthouse or online of your computer. But, the best way is word of mouth through the old family grapevine.

We have all suffered failures in life but, you have to "walk it off!" Grandma always told us if something goes wrong then get up and pull your pants up and quit crying over spilt milk and do something about it. There are so many of us who want to sit around and blame the other guy for something. But, we shouldn't act like that. Take responsibility for your own actions and when your wrong admit it and say your "sorry". It takes a bigger person to admit when they are wrong. So, build your own personal rules in life, but using perspective and compassion.

"Fear is a great inhibitor to healthy growth and complacency is the kiss of death."

Forgetting goes with forgiving. Once you forgive, you let it go. You don't bring it up ever again. Your grace will be rewarded in many ways both immediatley and in the long run.

Those ladies were adamant that you don't hold grudges. Holding on to a grudge will make your way cumbersome. They taught us to let by-gones be by-gones. You can lighten your heart when you wish no one any ill will. When you despise no one or blame no one, you'll be better off in the long run. You've got to love a critic. Someone to tell you what your faults are and your strengths. That's unconditional love.

"If it's an eye for an eye, then we would all be blind."

Give the people that you come across in your life a chance to present themselves to you fully. Try and find the best in them. Most everyone has something good in them to offer up. Even though, some you have to dig deep to find their good qualities and attributes. But, for the most part everyone has some good in them.

"You shouldn't judge a book by it's cover. But, always make sure that you have a nice book cover!"

We have all lost loved ones in our lives as well. And that feeling of loss is great. Sometimes after a period of personal trauma or unhappiness it's necessary to withdraw from the world for a little while so that the heart can heal faster. In order for the healing process to take place it's essential to withdraw for a little while. It is difficult to recover from physical or emotional pain while attempting to live normally as though nothin' has happened. We call this a period of mourning. This mourning process helps the soul to heal. Seems Southerners take this mourning process serious. Well, depending on how much they liked ya'.

At times you need to feel the pain. Wheather it be physical or mental. That's how you let yourself know that you are human. So, that way you can remember to remain or become humble.

Sorrow must be properly mourned in order to move on, only then will the release of the tension and strain give way to a more peaceful phase of life.

Sometimes life seems to be conspiring to thwart desires and wishes that we may have. Maybe, not in an especially destructive or even a vicious way, though. Obstacles in our path or maybe many small things can or will go wrong causing the cumaltive effect to result in extreme aggravation or frustration. This may be unpleasant but it's not life threatening. So, again I say; "Walk it Off!"

"Lay the groundwork. Create the dynamic that y'all may seek in your life. Small improvements may add up to big differences in your life."

Grandma told me once of an old English proverb that suggest that a full cup must be carried steadily. Take your time and move carefully through the day because your cup is more full than you realize.

"To be truly free you must be self reliant."

I found this geneology information from my family through the "Old Family Grapevine". My aunt, Jenna Lee used to tell me stories about three brothers who came over from England that were our family descendants. She said their names were Shadrach, Meshach and Abednego Inman, (biblical names from the bible). She said that our family line was branched off from Abednego Inman who settled in Dandridge, Tennessee.

So, being the investigator that I am, I looked into my geneology and she was right about it all. See how the family grapevine works?

It seems that through our family records that Shadrach, Meshach and Abednego Inman were also good friends with Daniel Boone who hailed from North Carolina. Daniel Boone was known as a "legend" in these parts. He was also a frontiersman and woodsman.

One of the earliest references we have to Abednego Inman is found in the "Missouri Historical Review Magazine", (Vol. 6, pg. 138-140, 1912).

"About the year 1767, a party of explorers left their homes in North Carolina to visit the vast and almost wholly unknown region lying West of the Cumberland Mountains. This party was led by Daniel Boone, who, at that early period had established a well deserved reputation for daring and a consummate knowledge of woodcraft. In this company there were three brothers who bore the scriptural names of Shadrach, Meshach and Abednego Inman, the first of whom was the Great-Grandfather of the writer hereof Gray and Bradford.

In due season they crossed the mountain range lying in the path of travel and winter soon swept down upon them. For days they pushed forward through deep snows. They had little or no food during this time for that which they had brought with them had been exhausted. They were, therefore, compelled to depend upon such game for their subsistence as they could bring down with their rifles, and killing game at that time of the year was not always easily accomplished.

When they arrived near the central part of the state of Tennessee and were encamped near a cave, probably the famous Nick-a-Jack Cave. They were surprised and attacked one night by Indians. Being asleep at the time of the attack, and not having taken the precaution to post sentinels, nearly all the little band of adventurers were either killed or wounded.

Among the slain was Meshach Inman. Among the wounded were Shadrach and his brother Abednego. The former recieved a wound in the side from a spear, which weapon is still in existence and in the possession of one of his descendants. Abednego recieved a wound in the forehead from an Indian tomahawk, leaving a scar. Which he carried for the remainder of his life.

Surviving his wound he placed himself in hiding in a large hollow tree, where he remained for nine days without food and with but a little water, at the end of which period he was so far recovered as to be able to leave his strange habitation and eventually with extreme difficulty he made his way back to his home in North Carolina. At this time Abednego could not have been over 16 years of age.

The company was thus broken up and dispersed and the expedition abandoned. Among the number of those who escaped were Boone and Shadrach Inman. Boone on account of his superior skill and woodcraft and knowledge of the Indian wiles escaped unharmed and returned home. The Indians pursued him keenly through the dense forest but, like a fleeting shadow he eluded them and led the few survivors of his little company safely back to their home.

Notwithstanding these misfortunes, our brave adventurers were not to be diverted from their purpose of exploring and taking possesion of the soil of Tennessee for some of them returned to the locality at a later date and established themselves in the wilds of Boonesbourough and Bryant's Station.

Now, I guess I know why I have an adventuress soul. Remember, Grandpa Talley taught our family that there are sufficient inner resources that may be drawn upon when life is at it's most demanding. Well, so did Abednego, Shadrach and Meshach Inman.

Look into your own geneology and who knows what you will find. You may have come from Kings and Queens or you may be related to me, just an 'ole "Hillbilly".

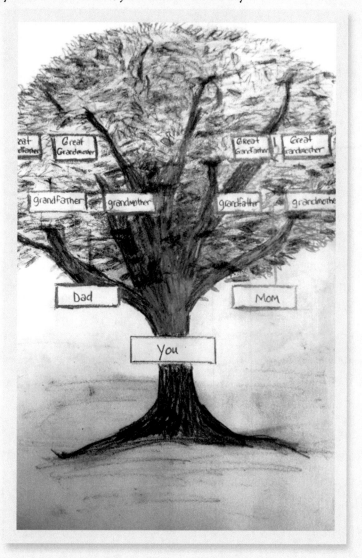

Chapter Ten

I promised you the directions on how to make yourselves a nice pipin' hot cornbread for your family and friends before we leave the kitchen. So, now let's get all of our necessary skillets, bowls, measuring cups and ingredients together so we'll have everything that we'll need to prepare it.

Our choices are: Regular cornbread, Sweet cornbread, Jalapino cornbread and a "Mexican" cornbread.

How to make a Regular cornbread:

Turn your oven on broil while you prepare your skillet and your batter.

Put one cup of oil (your choice of oil) in a medium to large size "seasoned" skillet and put it in the oven. (By the time that you have mixed your batter together your oil should be pipin' hot.)

Put three (3) cups of white or yellow stoneground cornmeal (self-rising) optional) in your bowl along with one (1) large egg, 1/2 tsp salt, 1 tsp baking powder, 1/4th cup of sour cream, (if useing buttermilk then omit the sour cream), one (1) cup of beer (beer helps it to rise and gives it a good flavor, the alcohol will cook out.) and 1/4 cup of warm water and 1/2 cup of whole milk.

Now, mix your batter until all of the cornmeal is wet. Turn your oven temperature down to 450' degrees on bake. Pour your batter into your skillet and bake for fifteen minutes. Don't forget to wear your potholders!

If you would prefer you may want a Sweet cornbread. Just use the same directions and add 1/4 cup of granulated sugar to your batter. Most of my family and friends prefer it sweet probably because they're so sweet.

Do you like a little "pep" in your step?

If you do then add either a half cup or a whole cup of chopped jalapino peppers to your batter for a Jalapino cornbread. You can't just serve that cornbread to anyone, though. I eat jalapino peppers all of the time and I hardly ever get a cold!

How to make a "Mexican" cornbread:

Use the same directions for your Regular or Sweet cornbread. Then add a 1/2 cup of chopped vadalia onions, 1/2 cup of sweet green and/or red bell peppers, 1/2 cup of whole kernel corn (drained) to your batter. After baking you'll have a colorful and tasty "Mexican" cornbread to add to any of your spicy recipes.

After your cornbread has cooled down then get a plate and flip your bread on it. Or, you can cut your cornbread right out of the skillet to serve from.

Always remember to wipe your skillet out to clean it so that you'll always have a "seasoned" skillet.

You may want to add some butter to your slice of cornbread while it's still warm.

If there is any cornbread left after your supper, remember how my Momma crumbled it up in a cup and poured milk on it for her dessert.

Sometimes if I have any cornbread left over the next day I will put a warm slice in a bowl with some cooked ground beef, add chopped onions, tomatoes and jalapino peppers with some of my home-made salsa and I've just made myself, my version of a "Hillbilly" tamale.

Now, if your in a hurry and want a quick supper try my "Cornbread Cassarole".

Make your cornbread batter and set it aside. Then brown some ground beef or ground turkey in a skillet. Drain off the grease. Add 1/4 cup of chopped green peppers, 1/4 cup of chopped onions, a can of green beans (drained), a can of whole kernel corn (drained) and a can of tomato sauce or a can of stewed tomatoes. Stir all of the ingredients together and simmer on top of the stove for five (5) minutes. Pour into a casserole dish and with a spoon top it with your cornbread batter until covered. (You probably won't use all of your cornbread batter.) Bake your cassarole until the cornbread topping is nice and brown (about 8 to 10 minutes). Oven temperature for this dish should be around 400' degrees on bake. Then remove your cassarole from the oven and now you've got a beautiful supper for you and your family and friends to enjoy!

Betty Jo's Hushpuppy recipe:

You can use a deep fryer, black iron Dutch oven or a deep pot to fry up your hushpuppies. Pour the oil of your choice in your pot and get it pipin' hot. In a large mixing bowl put in 3 cups of self-rising cornmeal, 1 cup of self-rising flour, 1 cup of fish fry batter (optional), 1 large onion diced fine, 1 large bell pepper diced fine, 1 can of whole kernel corn (drained), 1 cup of buttermilk. Then add enough beer to make the batter the right consistency to deep fry in hot oil (around 6 ounces or half a bottle of beer). Take some of the batter in your hand and make a ball, then drop it in your oil. I usually put two or three in the pot at a time. Your hushpuppies will float to the top and you can turn them around and around until they are golden brown. Take each one out with your tongs and put them in a separate bowl with a paper towel in it to absorb the excess oil.

Now, they are ready to eat. If you are wanting a stuffed hushpuppy then when you have your ball of batter in your hand stick a couple of already cooked shrimp inside each one. Yum, yum.

Here are some "Hillbilly" cuisine recipes from my brother, Mike's kitchen.

Mike's Rainbow trout recipe:

First catch a trout!

Mike says to first pop the eyes out from your trout. (Catfish can be prepared the same way.) Usually, a "Rainbow" trout or Catfish are prepared and served whole. Or, you can cut the heads off.

Then gut 'em and gill 'em.

Prepare your black iron skillet with 1/2 cup of oil.

(Your choice of oil) on medium heat.

In a bowl add 3/4 cups of cornmeal, a 1/4 cup of flour

Add (1) large egg (up to 3-4 fish)

Add (1) can of beer

Add salt and pepper to taste

Mix all ingredients and trout (catfish) in a brown paper bag and shake.

Then fry them on one side then turn the fish over and fry the other side on medium to low heat. The meat will be flaky when done.

Mike's Turtle Meat Recipe:

Soak your turtle meat in salted water while you prepare your ingredients.

Recipe is for 1lb to 3lb's of turtle meat.

Use a deep sided cast iron skillet with a lid.

In a bowl add 1/2 cup of flour and 1/2 cup of cornmeal.

Add one (1) large egg, 1/2 cup of buttermilk. (Buttermilk makes it crispy.)

Cook until golden brown on all sides.

After removing turtle meat from skillet leave crispies in the oil and add two spoonfulls of flour, salt and pepper to taste and stir with a fork to make your gravy.

After browning flour in all of the left over oil and crispies then add 3/4 cup of milk and stir again.

Suggested side dishes are bisquets for your gravy and a can of whole tomatoes.

Yummy!

Chapter Eleven

How to speak Southern:

A dialect is the form of a spoken language from a particular area. Down South we call our dialect a "Southern draw" or a "Southern accent". I'll have to say that we do have a way with words.

To this day I still can't understand why other people from other places have a problem with understanding what we're saying. We're talking as slow as we can and we even throw in a few more syllables to "draw" a word out. But, I do admit that with some words we take a few consonants out when we feel like they're not necessary. So, I guess there lies the problem, y'all.

"You have to have tolerance for the unorthodox. There is a special joy that comes from odd or unusal people all over the world."

If you ever get down to "My Neck of the Woods", then you may want to pay attention because I'm going to help y'all out. Here are some Southern sayings that you may hear while your visiting down yonder and with my help you may understand what those nice folks are saying or at most, trying to say.

(1.)   "How's your Mom and 'em?"
       How is your Mom and them (family)?
       Always ask about the family and how they are doing.

(2.)   "Come on in and sit for a spell."
       Come in and sit down for a short period of time.
       'Cause you don't want to wear out your welcome.

(3.)   "Well, Bless your heart."
       Something endearing to say to someone that you care about, especially babies.

(4.)   "Your barking up the wrong tree."
       This is something that is said if someone has misunderstood or they are totally wrong about a matter.

(5.)   "Hillbilly" swearin' words; Darn it, oh heck, shoot far, dang it and shucks.
       These words won't make your Momma or God mad at ya.

(6.)   "We're fixin' to go down yonder."

fixin'- getting ready (Seems Southerner's are always fixin' to do somethin'!)

down yonder-over there, down there.

(7.) "We're making cornbread and all of the fixins' to go with it."

Fixins' are other pre-pared food items to go with your main dish.

(8.) Y'all can stay until the "cows come home".

Seems cows like to roam the pastures to graze by day and make their way back home by the evening hours. You can't always count on that so sometimes you may have to send out one of the kids to call for them.

(9.) I wouldn't spit on you if you were on fire!

If you hear this saying when your down South then you've really made someone mad at ya'!

(10.) I've got to study on it.

This means before you get a straight forward answer. They're going to think about it for awhile. So, I wouldn't wait too long because, by the time they're ready to discuss the matter at hand it's been long forgotten. (That's called a reprieve!) (A post-ponement of an execution!)

I can't give you all of those Southern sayings, though. Heck, half of them I have to think twice about myself! But, if you hear something that you don't understand usually you can get the gist (main point) of it by the way they're saying it or the way that they look at you.

Now, while your running around those hollers and hills, well, you had better mind your manners. You say; "Thank You" and "Your Welcom'" when your in the South and in the presence of the elder folks, especially. They don't take kindly to rude or unruly behavior from anyone.

"Proper manners and ettiquete is; Not bringing attention to yourself. It's also an appropriate and cheerful interaction between folks."

In my family we had better mind our manners. We were taught to say, "Thank you" and "Your Welcom'" to be courtious and respectful always.

Wherever you come from you should always respect your elders. As children we were also taught to not call our elders by their first names. You use a title of respect in front of their given name such as; Aunt Jenna Lee or Uncle Ed.

And as your driving around East Tennessee and enjoying your surroundings please be nice enough to wave back at those sweet folks. Seems everywhere that you go they're waving at you and smiling. They are extremely polite!

If you walk into one of their establishments they'll soon greet you with a "Hi, how ya doin'?". And it's just polite to greet them back with saying, "Fine, how are you?". It's the neighborly way around here folks.

If your in need of directions well, good luck. You may want to invest in a navigational system or GPS for your vehicle because Southerners have their own way of giving directions. It's the old-timey way of direction using landmarks. Any prominent feature on the land will do.

For example, they may say to you; "Go down yonder aways until you see a big oak tree then turn the corner and go down there aways until you see the red barn (the other barns are gray). When you get to the red barn and look up the hill there sittin' beside that old tractor is the gas pumps at our only "country" store around these parts. "Good luck folks and have a nice day!"

Hey, don't run into me and ask me for directions. I couldn't get my way out of a paper bag with the directions wrote on it!

Thinking back on my up-bringing, I'd have to say that those "Hillbillies" did a pretty good job raising all of us kids for the most part. God sticks ya where he wants ya. I truly believe that. Appreciate where your from. I could have been born and raised in Australia and running around with one of those "Aussie" accents. But no, he chose the South for me.

He also chose some wonderful people to raise me. We were well taught to be up-standing people. Even though we may be a little rough around the edges, we turned out to be good natured, friendly, honest and forthright people.

So, listen up while your down South. You may learn something that you didn't know that you needed to learn.

"We could all use a good lesson every now and then."

Chapter Twelve

We've learned a lot in my Grandma's kitchen so far but, we still have a lot more to learn. We've learned a little bit about life and a little bit about cookin'. Now, I'm going to give y'all some other lessons on some Southern sayings and what they mean so pay attention!

Southern Sayings:

(1.) I'm skinnin' this cat, you just hold it's tail.
       (I'm in charge so you just help out.)

(2.) The apple dosen't fall to far from the tree.
       (The child is like his Momma or his Daddy.)

(3.) I'm happier than a pig in slop.
       (I'm very happy, elated.)

(4.) I brought you into this world and I can take you out!
       (Something that your Momma or your Daddy would say if you are in real big trouble.)

(5.) He's madder than a hornet's nest.
       (He's very mad.)

(6.) He's fit to be tied.
       (He's really mad.)

(7.) Flying off the handle.
       (A violent explosion of temper. To loose one's self control.)

(8.) Having a chip on one's shoulder.
       (Put a chip of wood on your shoulder and if someone knocks it off then the fight is on!)

(9.) Burry the hatchet.
       (To make peace after someone's made you madder than a hornet's nest.)

(10.) Like white on rice!
        (Getting as close as you can to someone or something or you are on top of the situation.)

(11.) You can't get blood out of a turnip.
        (This means that you can't get something from nothing.)

(12.) Well, Bless your heart and Bless your soul.

(We wish you the best.)

(13.) Better than a poke in the eye with a sharp stick.

(Some things are better than nothing.)

(14.) No skin off my back.

(Nothing's that bad.)

(15.) Right now, in a minute.

(Oxymoron- A figure of speech in which contradictory terms are combined.)

(16.) You're getting on my last nerve.

(I'm about done with the situation at hand.)

(17.) You've got to choose your own battles.

(Sometimes the fight is not worth it!)

(18.) He is in high cotton.

(Someone who thinks he is rich or better than someone else.)

(19.) Livin' high on the hog.

(Someone who tries to get everything and tries to take everything that you have.)

(20.) Opened a whole can of worms.

(Too much information or causing a conflict.)

(21.) The short end of the stick. No matter how long the stick is.

(Someone who seems to always fall short of others.)

(22.) Take a stab at it.

(Give it a shot or give it a try.)

(23.) I feel like a stuffed hog.

(I've eaten too much.)

(24.) I wouldn't touch it with a ten foot pole.

(You don't want to involve yourself in the situation at hand at all.)

(25.) "Hang in there!"

("You can't kill a man born to hang!")

(26.)   Okey Dokey

(Yes, No problem.)

(27.)   Down in the Boondocks

(Living in a wild or wooded area.)

(28.)   Pull him up by his boot straps.

(Most of the boots had straps on either side so, if you hear that expression, then he needed some help with pulling him out of somethin'.)

(29.)   Misery loves company.

(People that are not in a good way who want to be with other people that arn't in a good way.)

(30.)   I'll let you sleep with the dogs.

(Your threatening someone that they can't keep good company with you.)

Well, have you learned anything so far? And have you heard any of these Southern sayings before? If you have then maybe, you've got a "Southerner" in the "wood pile". That means that one of your relatives may have been a "Southerner"!

Here are some more Southern sayings that you may have heard before while your scratching your head and trying to figure out who the "Southerner" in the family is.

(31.)   Simmer down now.

(Become quiet or relaxed.)

(32.)   He ain't got sense enough to come in out of the rain.

(He's not very smart, kind of stupid.)

(33.)   I'll give you a peice of my mind.

(To tell someone off.)

(34.)   Eyes are the window to the soul.

(Look into someone's eyes to see if they look you straight in the eyes. Then if they look you straight in the eyes back they may be telling the truth about somethin'!)

(35.)   Don't get your nose out of joint.

(Don't get your feelings hurt.)

(36.)   He's running around like a chicken with his head cut off.

(He's acting kind of crazy.)

(37.) He's too big for his britches.

(He thinks to highly of himself.)

(38.) He may take a shine to ya'.

(To like someone.)

(39.) He has an axe to grind.

(A grievance that has lasted along time. Could be hostile or combative.)

(40.) Tit for Tat.

(Is the same meaning as the Latin version of; Quid Pro Quo. Which means; You do something for me and I'll do something for you.) The "Southern" version is; "You scratch my back and I'll scratch yours!"

(41.) Don't ruffle his feathers.

(Don't get someone riled up.)

(42.) You're in a pickle.

(It means that your in a mess or a bad situation.)

(43.) Your cup is half full.

(It means: Go through your day carefully 'cause your cup may be more full than you realize.)

(44.) Like a rock.

(Somethin' is solid.)

(45.) Scratch your head.

(Think about it for awhile.)

(46.) There is always a few bad apples in a bunch.

There is always at least one person in a group of people that is "no count".)

(47.) They don't know "Shit from Shinola".

(The only shoe polish back in those days was Shinola. Well, they compared it to ....)

(48.) Between you and me and the fence post.

Whatever your saying is between you and me, basically.)

(49.) Don't bite off more than you can chew.

(Don't say too much in case you can't handle the repercussion.)

(50.)   Don't count your chickens before they are hatched.

Don't assume that all of your plans will turn out.)

Now, that's plenty of Southern sayings for you to think about for awhile. But, while your thinkin' have you figured out who the "Southerner" in the "wood pile" is, yet?

Chapter Thirteen

Southern Rhetoric (The art of using words effectively.):

(1.)   Y'all - Ye all, You all.

(2.)   Yeah - Yes

(3.)   Yokel - A person from the country.

(4.)   Countrified - Having the appearance of rural or country people.

(5.)   Country bumpkin - An awkward or backward person from the country.

(6.)   Hick - An unsophisticated or simple person.

(7.)   Whoopin' - To whip or to strike as with a strap.

(8.)   Hooch - Home-made liquor.

(9.)   Ne'er do well - A good for nothing person.

(10.)   Poke - A paper bag

(11.)   Neck of the woods - The area where someone lives and/or where they are from.

(12.)   Ain't - Is not

(13.)   Hankerin' - A desire or longing for something.

(14.)   Snipe/Snipe Hunting - The dictionary says; A Snipe is a long billed wading bird. But, where I come from it's a fictional animal that we take our kids to look for that they are never going to find!

(15.)   Britches - Pants

(16.)   Kin - Related by bloodline (Consanguineous). A relative.

(17.)   "Hightail it" - Move fast, fullspeed

(18.)   Backwoods - Someone from a remote or underveloped area.

(19.)   Trailblazing - Marking paths. For example, putting markings on trees that follow each other in the direction of the trail.

(20.)   Pig Pickin' - A party. (It is basically just a Southern barbeque or a party outside. It is nice though, if someone brings a pig to barbeque!)

(21.)   Rabbit food - Eatin' lettuce or vegetables.

(22.) Buggy - It's what us Southerners call a shopping cart. Or it is a horse with a cart behind it.

(23.) Toboggan - A knitted, fitted hat or a sleigh to coast down the hill in the snow with.

(24.) Pipe down - Quiet down

(25.) Hen party - That is what we call a bunch of the women folk getting together.

(26.) Spell - A brief period of time.

(27.) Lordy mercy - From; Oh Lord have mercy.

(28.) Don't shut the door - When one door closes another door opens.

(29.) Act up - Misbehaving

(30.) Every which way - In all directions

Well, how's your lesson going so far? If you liked that Southern rhetoric then here are some more to scratch your head over.

(31.) Apple peeler - A pocket knife

(32.) Fair to middlin' - Feeling pretty good

(33.) Get shed of - Get rid of

(34.) Hoppin' mad - Very angry

(35.) Hush up - Shut your mouth

(36.) Kitchen safe - Kitchen cupboard

(37.) Pie safe - A cupboard with open grates on the doors to let air in to store your pies.

(38.) Jawin' - Talking a lot

(39.) Have one's druthers - Have one's desires

(40.) Jump over the broom stick - To get married or hitched.

(41.) Lay a hand on - To hit someone

(42.) Crick - Creek or little stream

(43.) Fussed over - To make a big deal over something or someone.

(44.) Lap baby - An infant

(45.) He's a "card" - Someone special or unique

(46.) Play possum - To play dead

(47.) Set up with - Sitting with someone who is sick.

(48.) He's no count - Good for nothin'

(49.) Rambunctious - Starting trouble

(50.) Narin' - None

(51.) No how - Anyhow

(52.) Laid eyes on y'all - Looked at you

(53.) A rite smart - A lot of something

(54.) The law - The sheriff

(55.) Shing-dig - A party or pig-pickin'

(56.) Piddle - Wasting time

(57.) Piddlin' - A small amount

(58.) Rot gut liquor - Bad liquor

(59.) Swig - A small drink

(60.) The whole kit and kaboodle - The entire amount

(61.) Slue - A large amount

(62.) Smidgen - A small amount

(63.) Puny - Sickly

(64.) Dope - Coke

(65.) To sop - To soak up with bread.

(66.) Sho'nuff - Sure enough

(67.) Sashay - To strut around like a peacock.

(68.) To shuck - To take something off.

(69.) You can't take it with ya when ya go - Give up your belongings.

(70.) Evil eye - I've got my eye on ya.

You can't say that us Southerners don't have a knack with our words. We've also got a lot of unique phrases too.

Wherever you hail from wheather it be New York, Massachusetts, Maine or Texas with their slang, seems everyone has a way with words.

I love accents. If you listen closely enough you can peg someone's origin just by the way that they talk. They say that; "Birds of a feather flock together." Which means; people with like traits and/or taste. People have always wanted to be with their own kind. Some however; have ventured out an adapted to other types of people and have faired well with them. Learning some of their ways and some even picking up on their accents.

"Unburden your mind and set yourself free."

Here are some more phrases that are truly unique:

(1.)   Mean as a striped snake.

(2.)   Wild as a buck.

(3.)   Mad as a wet hen.

(4.)   Dumb as an ox.

(5.)   Crazy as a loon.

(6.)   Blind as a bat.

(7.)   Clumsy as an ox.

(8.)   Sly as a fox.

(9.)   Fat as a hog.

(10.)   Thin as a rail.

(11.)   Broad as a barn.

(12.)   Grinnin' like a possum (o'possum).

(13.)   Happy as a lark.

(14.)   Proud as a peacock.

(15.)   Fat as a tub of lard.

(16.)   Flat as a pancake.

(17.)   Naked as a jaybird.

(18.)   Smart as a whip.

(19.)   Right as rain.

(20.)   Cool as a cucumber.

(21.)   Hot as fire.

(22.)   Dry as a bone.

(23.) Hot as a firecracker.

(24.) Low as a snake.

(25.) Dull as dishwater.

(26.) Sharp as a tack.

(27.) Bright as a new penny.

(28.) Dead as a doorknob.

(29.) Wet as a drowned rat.

(30.) Take a shine to.

(31.) Lyin' like a rug.

(32.) Deep as the ocean.

(33.) Hard as a nail.

(34.) Stiff as a board.

(35.) Limber as a dishrag.

(36.) Soft as a baby's bottom.

(37.) Sweet as honey.

(38.) Sweet as a cherry pie.

(39.) Ugly as home-made sin.

(40.) Pretty as a speckled puppy.

(41.) Drunk as a skunk.

(42.) Sober as a judge.

(43.) High as a kite.

(44.) Clean as a whistle.

(45.) Down yonder aways.

(46.) Poor as a churchmouse.

(47.) Quiet as a churchmouse.

(48.) Fit to be tied.

(49.) Faster than lightnin'.

(50.) Pull the wool over my eyes.

All of these "Southern" sayings and "Southern" rhetoric are words that you may have heard in your life time or you may not have heard any of them. Down South we say; There's no normal life, there's just life. So, relax and have some fun.

"Stop your hemmin' and hawin' and sit back and enjoy the ride."

Chapter Fourteen

Some Things That I Learned In My Grandma's Kitchen:

(1.)   You reap what you sow.

(2.)   It's never too late to heal the soul.

(3.)   If you choose hope then anything is possible.

(4.)   I suppose that hope is patient.

(5.)   Think carefully and impartially.

(6.)   Family; "From the womb to the tomb."

        "Forever woven into the fabric."

        "Water is sweet but, blood is thicker."

(7.)   Honey is sweet, but the bees sting.

(8.)   Nothing goes to Heaven until something leaves the Earth.

(9.)   The great burial church the Earth is.

(10.)   Life is for the living, "Embrace every moment."

(11.)   Once you know something then you can never unknow it.

(12.)   Don't drive or ride faster than your guardian angel can fly.

(13.)   Being alone isn't the same as being lonely.

(14.)   You have never met anyone by accident.

(15.)   Strength is control rather than destruction.

(16.)   If fear can be overcome and positive action taken then matters can improve.

(17.)   It's funny how time slips away. So, enjoy the day!

(18.)   Breathe in for the rise and exhale for the fall. That is sure to give you happiness again and again.

(19.)   There are no measures for personal success that are constant, because personal success is different for everyone. Work hard and be your best, that will be your true success.

(20.)   There are many reasons why it would be better to settle into your humanity than to strive for perfection. The reception you will get will be friendlier because no one can relate to perfection at all.

(21.)   Excellence doesn't happen overnight. You must rise to a level of excellence in any situation.

(22.)   If you believe in Karma; It will come around for those who have wronged you. Sometimes, the universe will balance out the scales for you.

(23.)   People want to give you advice but, the best advice will be an inside message sent from your heart to your head, (you'll know).

(24.)   The power of positive mind thinking:
        If you think negative, negative will transpire.
        If you think positive, positive will transpire.
        So, keep a positive attitude.

(25.)   Build yourself up, don't underestimate what you can do.

(26.)   Take educated risks and move forward for a brighter future.

(27.)   Never apologize for another person's behavior, otherwise you could be an enabler.

(28.)   Making the point to be heard is important for your self-esteem.

(29.)   Only the truly powerful are brave enough to throw consequence to the wind.

(30.)   Sadness and grief, it's clear that there is still hope. It denotes regret and sorrow but, it is not without hope or expectations.

(31.)   Strong and wrong will rule over weak and right everytime.

(32.)   Memories are important but, don't live too much in the past.

(33.)   Every adventure involves the elements of danger. No danger, no excitement. No excitement, no fun!

(34.)   Sacrifices have to be made in life, so prepare yourself to make them.

(35.)   The long and winding road in life that fools you at every turn. So, keep your course!

(36.)   A lesson of solitude, which is often one man's greatest fear. Once the truth of aloneness is faced it stops being so frightening.

(37.)   Evaluation and self assessment: Summing up and balancing emotional accounts by looking over your recent past.

(38.)   Invest in your life! Set your priorities! (Remember Grandpa Talley set his priorities; God first, family, work and then everything else that is important to you.)

(39.) The enjoyment of the fruits of all our labor, the profound sense of satisfaction that can be found through effort. (Example; Maybe the simple pleasure of eating a piece of fruit that you have grown yourself.)

(40.) There are times in life when the best course of action is to swallow our pride and walk away from difficult situations.

(41.) Don't let your left hand know what your right hand is doing. Example; Do a good deed and say nothing about that good deed that you did.

(42.) The gift of gab is both a blessing and a curse.

(43.) Angry people talk faster than they think and say things that they do not really mean at times.

(44.) Honor your body and sharpen your mind.

(45.) Carry another on your back but, only carry those who truly need the lift.

(46.) The power of the mind can be well used to make clear and impartial decisions.

(47.) Diplomacy has it's time and place.

(48.) The family that prays together stays together.

(49.) Prayer will give you the answers that you need. So, humble yourself and listen.

(50.) Grandma's Prayer;

Dear Heavenly Father,

In accordance with thy gospel and in the name of Jesus Christ I pray that the Holy Spirit will;

Bless us with love, peace, happiness, good health, strength and prosperity.

Amen

"You start over everyday. One day at a time. Never give up."

Chapter Fifteen

Hillbilly Remedies:

Yellow Jaundice:

My son, Joseph was born three weeks early and the doctors told us that he had Yellow Jaundice. Yellow Jaundice refers to the yellow color of the skin and whites of the eyes caused by excess bilirubin in the blood. Bilirubin is produced by the normal breakdown of red blood cells.

In high levels of Jaundice, phototherapy helps rid the body of the bilirubin by altering it or making it easier for your baby's liver to get rid of it. Which is what my doctor suggested that we do. So, he wanted to put him in the hospital and put him through the phototherapy treatment.

We had to wait three days after Joseph was diagnosed to put him in the hospital to use the phototherapy treatment on him. Well, Grandma Mollie said, "Give me that baby!". So, I did. She stripped him naked and put him in his baby carrier and put him up by her window so that the sun could shine in on him. She did that process for a few days. There he was naked as a Jaybird peeing in the wind when necessary. That kept me laughing as nervous as I was at the time. Momma and I took him to his scheduled appointment three days later to put him in the hospital to let the doctor's do what they do best. When I got him there the doctor took me aside and said, "I don't know what you did but, that baby doesn't have Yellow Jaundice anymore, at all!" Well, thank the Lord for those Southern Grandmas and their Southern remedies!

After this happened with my son Joseph, I started to think about what other "Hillbilly" remedies Grandma had up her sleeve. So, I started asking questions and boy, did I learn a lot. I'd like to share some of these "Hillbilly" remedies with y'all. Maybe, you can use some for yourself or your family and friends.

You know back then they didn't have a pharmacy at every corner and a lot of people couldn't or wouldn't go to the doctor because they didn't have that much money. So, they had to rely on "Tried and True" methods to get themselves through it. Usually, those methods were passed down from their generation to our generation.

Ear ache:

My Grandma would do one or two things to cure our ear aches. She would put a little bit of olive oil in our ear and a cotton swab and/or sometimes she would blow smoke from a cigarette in our ear and seal that with a cotton swab. Either way right afterwards we could hear again and our ears didn't ache anymore.

Jellyfish or Man-of-War stings:

While vacationing in Myrtle Beach, South Carolina once with my family when I was a child I remember my Daddy was swimming in the ocean and was stung by a Man-of-War. The Man-of-War and the Sea Nettle have a more serious and more painful sting than a jellyfish. These stings should recieve serious medical attention. However; when out on a secluded beach and when your in a lot of serious pain sometimes you have to do what you have to do.

My Dad immediatley urinated on his stings to relieve the pain until we got back to our place where he then used vinager to add to his relief. After this happened he explained to my brothers and I that by urinating and using the vinager on the stings added salts and electrolytes to the infected area. He then coated his legs and feet with shaving cream to make a paste over the infected areas where he was stung.

Don't ask me where he learned this self healing technique. All I know is he knew what to do and acted immediatley to cure the problem. He also taught my brothers and I how to re-act in a situation like that. I've heard that in Australia where they have an abundance of Man-of War and jellyfish attacks that they have mailboxes up and down their coast filled with vinager inside for emergencies just like this.

Heartburn, Stomach ache and Sea sickness:

If you've got heartburn or a stomach ache then Grandma would fill a cup of soda water and a spoonful of bitters to it. She would then tell us to drink the concoction as fast as we could ('cause it doesn't taste very good). Well, after we drank it the heartburn or our up-set stomachs would be gone.

(Bitters was introduced to us in the early 1800's. The ingredients are aromatic herbs, bark, roots and/or fruit for their flavor and medicinal properties.)

Grandma's use of this remedy cured her children and her grand-children of heart-burn and stomach aches. I was also told that it had cured my Grandfather Ralph of his seasickness back when he was a child.

Hiccups:

Grandma's remedy to cure hiccups is to use bitters on a slice of lemon. Pour a half of spoonful of bitters on a slice or two of lemon and suck it. It will immediatley cure your hiccups.

Gastritis:

Put a few drops of bitters in warm water and drink. (Or add to your coffee or orange juice.) Take before a meal to encourage the gastrontestinal system to release the hormone gastrin, which increases gastric acid, bile and other digestive secretions. Or take after a meal if the meal is not agreeing with you. This will immediatley cure your problem.

Toothache:

Back in the day dentist were out of the question. No money! Grandma would put a little whiskey on our gums to ease or dull the pain until a dentist was available or other means were sought!

Baby's teething:

She also put a little bit of whiskey on the baby's gums to ease or dull the pain while they were teething. Not a lot! All this did was numb the area of pain.

Another remedy for treating a toothache temporarily until other means were sought was to take a teabag and heat it in hot water then take the teabag and place it on the tooth or infected gum. It will draw out the infection.

Bee stings:

Grandma would take snuff or cigarette tobacco and wet it to apply to the infected area. That would dull the sting and the pain.

Baby rash:

Grandma would take dry cornstarch and rub it on the rash to ease the pain. This also works for athelete's feet and other skin rashes such as heat rash.

Denise Carberry's German family recipe for cough medicine:

Take two large onions and cut thin slices. Put the thin slices of onions in a shallow bowl and add one (1) cup of sugar to cover the onions. Press mixture with a heavy iron lid. Let mixture sit for a few hours until a juice is produced. The juice can be used for a cough medicine.

Grandma's "Hillbilly" cough medicine recipe:

3/4 cup of honey

1/4 cup olive oil

3 or 4 lemons (juiced)

For flavor you can add cinnamin or vanilla extract for they are both antiflamitory to sore throats. If you are treating a child under the age of one, then use molasses instead of honey. Heat your ingredients over the stove on medium heat until mixture comes to a boil. Cool to a medium temperature then serve a few spoonfuls to your loved one as necessary. You can put the rest in a jar and can it for future use.

Grandma's Hot toddy recipe:

A hot toddy is good to treat a cold, the flu or a sore throat. It will help with the aches and pains and relax you. It will also break-up the inflammation, as well.

How to make a "Hot toddy":

Boil one teabag in a cup of hot water. Then add the juice of half a lemon. Add two (2) spoonfulls of honey. Add two (2) spoonfulls of whiskey or bourbon. (you can add a little cinnamin or ginger if you have it). Mix the concoction and sip it all down. This toddy will relax you and make you feel better.

Grandma's easy sore throat gargle:

Add a teaspoon of salt to a glass of warm water (if you have sage leaves add a few of them to your mixture). Then gargle. Grandma used good old salt for a lot of cure-alls. She would take Epson's salt and add to warm water to soak your aching feet as well.

Tick bites:

We used to play outside a lot and if we ever showed up with a tick on us Grandma would apply vasaline to the tick and our skin which would cause the tick to stop breathing. After removing the tick check to make sure the head is still attached then burn the tick and the tick head.

Sunburn:

Take the leaf from an aloe plant and cut in half then rub the liquid fom the leaf on your sunburn and let it dry naturally. Continue the process as needed or until you run out of leaves.

You can also make a paste of baking soda and water to apply to your skin to ease the burn. Lye soap is another remedy. Just lather the lye soap up and apply to skin and let dry.

Grandma used lye soap for just about everything. She used it for cleaning and washing clothes. She didn't make it herself, though. She would get it from another "Hillbilly" relative who used to make it. Grandma swore by it. She said that it wasn't just for cleaning the household or doing her laundry but, it was medicinal too. Here are a list of problems that lye soap can cure:

Dry skin, acne, skin rashes (psoriasis and exzema), poison ivy, poison oak, mosquito bites, chigger bites, sunburn, athelete's feet, lice and fleas on pets.

If you get a chance to purchase some lye soap I would recommend it (I keep it in my household and use it all of the time).

Hot peppers, onions and garlic:

Hot peppers have "Capsaicin" in them which has a healing effect on respiratory problems. Capsaicin helps lungs function more effectively. (Great news for smokers!). They have a high source of vitamin C. By eating hot peppers consistantly it can help with asthma and breathing problems, sinus and nasal conditions and other respiratory illnesses.

Onions have a compound called "Quercetin" in them which is an antioxidant agent. Onions boost the good type of cholesterol (HDL) in your body. They do their best work when eaten raw.

Garlic lowers cholestoral but, can raise the good type of cholestoral (HDL). We need the good cholestoral in our bodies just not the bad cholestoral. Garlic produces "natural killer" blood cells to help our bodies to tackle infections and tumors (which could be cancerous). It is best to eat it raw and often.

Pain management vs prescribed drugs:

Maybe, not every ailment but in a lot of cases instead of taking pills for your pain there are other ways to relieve your pain and stress. It might be easier to take a pill and it may be harder to try other remedies but, in my opinion the hard way is usually the best way.

Chicken soup as a cold and flu remedy:

Grandma always treated our cold or flu symptons with a nice bowl of her home-made chicken soup. (Chicken soup recipes vary.) It's a proven fact that a nice bowl of chicken soup provides emotional and psycological well-being to both adults and children. Whether you believe that chicken soup can cure the common cold or not. And it's also proven that there are ingredients in the chicken, chicken bone and the vegetables that you add to the soup (add as many vegetables as you can) all have medicinal qualities. For example; The chicken and chicken bones have carnosine, an antitoxidant. Also, the chicken bones after being cooked for awhile put out into the stock minerals like zinc, calcium, phosphorus and magnesium. And of course, the more vegetables the better. They put into the stock vitamins and minerals as well. That's more antioxidants to fight off your cold!

So, when you have a family member or a friend with a cold try and figure out how to whip them up a nice bowl of chicken soup if you really want to help!

Bad breath:

Sometimes, us kids would come up with a case of bad breath. And who better than Grandma to tell us about it and to help us with our problem? She would either have us chew on parsley sprigs or she would add parsley sprigs to hot water and add a little ginger root or ground cloves for us to gargle with. Thank you Grandma and thanks for feeding us all of that garlic, eew!

These "Hillbilly" remedies were used as a practice on my family and myself. By no means am I suggesting that these remedies will cure all that ails you. I am not a doctor and neither were my

Grandmothers. You can try these "Hillbilly" remedies if you want to but, I'm just saying that we're not doctors and you can't hold us to it!

When you've got a problem then anything is worth a try. Sometimes a "Hillbilly" remedy is better than an old doctor anyway!

"Just ask Grandma, she knows everything!"

Chapter Sixteen

You can take "this girl" out of those hollers, hills and mountains. And you can take me to the beach, (East coast or West coast). You can take me to the desert or even to a beautiful Bay area. But, I'm going to return back to those rolling hills every time. They have my heart and soul.

Those beautiful "Smokey" mountains are mine. They also belong to you. God gave them to us to enjoy in their majestic, raw beauty. Now, that's freedom! They are so beautiful and breath-taking that you may want to take the long way home.

It amazes me how some people who live in New York city for example, have never left a few blocks from their homes in their entire lifetime. I believe that the world is our oyster and we should try and see as much of it as we possibly can.

If you havn't started your "Bucket" list (things that you want to do before you ("Kick the Bucket"), you may want to get started. Time is a wastin'. Wasting away that is. Go see a relative or an old friend or a new friend. Road trips are pretty exciting. I've had many exciting road trips in my days. You never know what to expect or who you may meet. Remember Grandma Mollie said; "You never meet anyone by accident."

Set the course and see where it takes you. I'm pretty sure that you can find your way back home, (your "Tara" per se). And if you hop on an airplane and leave us for awhile try and not come home with one of those "Aussie" accents. A Southern draw wouldn't be too bad. At least I could understand ya!

"Before you set your sails, enjoy the breeze."

I'm not saying that you need to leave home forever. I'm saying have an adventuress soul. It's uplifting. It's just dang good for the soul to venture out. If you venture down South well, I believe that you'll be ok now that I have taught you how to speak and understand "Southern"! "Nothing ventured, nothing gained."

There is much to see in this great country that we call "America, Land of the Free". I have visited some amazing places in this country. I went and saw "The Painted Desert" near Holbrook, Arizona. Some people call it "nothingless" well, I beg to differ. For flatlanders, the view is amazing and wonderful.

It is a masterpiece of layers of soil and rock in beautiful colors of red, orange, yellow, pink and purple.

I've also visited the "Petrified Forest" which is something out of another time. The park was the home of Native Americans who built and occupied that part of America between 1,250 and 1,380 years ago before moving on.

Petrified wood is scattered throughout the park. Some of the wood or logs that you will see are over 200 million years old! That old wood has the appearance of new wood even though it has turned to stone. Scientists have found dinasaur skeletons more than 200 million years old from the Triassic period. Every crook and cranny has a dinasaur skeleton hidden somewhere.

My brother, David and I thought about taking a little souvenir home with us until we saw a sign that said, "Don't take any petrified wood or you will be prosecuted". Well, that scared the petrified wood right out of our pockets!

After that then we were on our way to the "Grand Canyon". A large canyon carved by the Colorado River in the state of Arizona. The "Grand Canyon" is kept and managed by the Grand Canyon National Park, The Hualapai tribal nation and the Havasupai tribe. It is 277 miles long and up to 18 miles wide. Now, just think about this perimeter. Have you ever seen anything like that before? Well, all you have to do is travel down Interstate 40 heading West. When you get there it's so enormous and vast that you may have to see it more than once to take it all in.

They will let you ride donkeys down the trails well into it or maybe you may choose to take a helicopter ride over it for a different perspective of it all. I just wish that I had spent a few more hours each time I was there to take it all in!

"It's just a "little" memory to put a "big" smile on your face."

The Hoover Dam is next after the Grand Canyon. You should view this magnificient, massive man made structure. It was built to irrigate the low lying plains, known as low desert areas. So, the United States government decided that the Colorado River was part of the solution to irrigate that part of the country. They will let you tour it and it could take all day to really take in what we can do when necessary. It is truly amazing.

I've been to Disney Land and have seen the California "Mickey Mouse" and I've been to Disney

World and have seen the Florida "Mickey Mouse". Of course, my favorite was the Southern "Mickey Mouse". You've got to love a mouse that says; "Hi! Y'all".

I've been up and down the coast of California and I fell in love with Marina Del Rey. I've never seen so many beautiful sailboats. But, I havn't had a desire yet to travel all the way to Alaska to see an igloo, (too cold!).

On one of my many "road trips" I took a ride up to Pahrump, Nevada. We watched a herd of wild horses running in the desert. That was probably one of my most joyful moments. Who can blame a girl, wild horses to watch, "Marshal Tucker" on the radio and riding shotgun beside a real cowboy! I miss that 'ole cowboy!

Now, for an old "Hillbilly" girl, New York city was pretty impressive. The Empire State building is 1,554 feet tall and we made it all the way to the top. It was like being on top of "Old Smokey". They sure don't make buildings like that down South. And the Statue of Liberty is a sight to behold. She is a majestic beauty.

If your feeling patriotic then you need to go to Washington, D.C. You can see the White House or visit some of many museums. Just don't get lost there. My husband and I saw the Washington Monument by every angle one night. I could not get him to stop for directions! What's that all about all you husbands out there?

Now are you gettin' what I'm trying to say? Try and have a little fun in life. Take a road trip and enjoy yourselves a little bit. If you can't get to Hawaii or to Key West, Florida, then maybe you can get down the road a little bit. It will be good for you. And wherever you go try to enjoy what those nice people that you meet are all about. Eat their food, listen to their music and try to understand what they are saying. And if they offer you some cornbread, well, hopefully their Grandma gave them the recipe!

Satisfy the senses by appreciating good food, good music, good quality materials and beauty in your surroundings. And try to share a quest for truth, beauty and love or try and cultivate these things in your heart. Tip your hat to this wonderful world that we all live in and let's walk side by side to see it.

"When you stop searching you loose the potential to know more. We do live in a world of wonder!"

The "Grand Canyon"

"The Painted Desert"
&
"The Petrified Forest"

The Definition of a Family or Kinfolk:
- (1.)   All of the people living in the same house. (Usually a Father and Mother and their children.)
- (2.)   Parents and their children (or any other relatives who may live with them).
- (3.)   Relatives-All the people that are related by blood.
- (4.)   Descended from a common ancestor.

The Definition of a Clan:
- (1.)   A group of families claiming the descent from a common ancestor.
- (2.)   A group of people with interests in common.

The Definition of God:
- (1.)   Any of various beings concieved of as supernatural, immortal and having special powers over people and nature.
- (2.)   An idol.
- (3.)   A person of thing deified.
- (4.)   In monatheism, the creator and ruler of the universe, eternal and all-powerful; Supreme being.

Chapter Seventeen

The family is a wonderful thing. If you have a family then you should embrace them. Down South you may hear "Family Clan" or "Kinfolk" but, it's all the same thing. We all try to stay together. We also try to take care of one another because that's what families do.

Back in the day the family depended upon one another for survival. The children would help their parents tend to their farms, farm animals or usually the family buisness. Wheather it was farming or whatever jobs that the family did for survival back in those days was what the children helped out with. The more children that a family had was more hands to help out with.

The parents taught their children with a hands on approach. They worked side by side to tackle their work and to get their jobs done efficiently. Hard work is good for the soul. There was no time for playing or messing around because things had to be tended to in order to put food on the table if you wanted to eat and have a place to live.

"Be content with what you have and what you have worked for. Contentment is the best action to take."

Having a lot of children back then supplied more hands to help out. They didn't use birth control back then because it wasn't necessary. The Father and the Mother accepted what the Good Lord blessed them with, as we should accept what he delivers to us. God has a plan for each of us and we should act on his plan accordingly. Don't try to change what God intends for you to have. He'll only give you what you can handle. So, some of us have to dig deeper than others, that's all.

"Genesis chapter 9, verse 7: And you, be ye fruitful, and multiply; bring forth abundantly in the earth, and multiply therin."

Everyone has a mother and father and some of us are lucky enough to have siblings. Listen to your parents for they only want the best for you, as God, our Father in heaven, only wants the best for you. And when in life if you have strife then get down on your hands and knees and pray to your Heavenly Father. He wants you to be happy. We all want you to be happy.

"Have humility and a willingness to change because your mind expands when you're in the presence of beauty. Lovliness helps you to see more possibilities for yourself and others."

Grandma Mollie and Grandma Kat told us how their families recognized their strengths and limitations (or weaknesses). They also said the best thing that you can give to your loved ones is space. Let them enjoy the time to do the things he or she finds so pleasurable. That's a gift to be cherished. Let them find their own way.

"You can't change people but, you can inspire them to change themselves. Show them strength and integrity and see how that enfolds."

I wanted to give you an idea of what a family really is. It is love, unconditional love. Just remember when you feel unloved that there is always someone in the family to turn to. And if that doesn't work for you then turn to your Heavenly Father. For those of you who do not believe in God then you really need to find a family member to turn to, because there is always someone there to help you.

Everyone needs someone to turn to when at some points in your life you need guidance or just human contact. We are all human and we all desire the same thing in life and that should be love and acceptance.

In the South we are what some people call the "Bible Belt". And, I do agree with that. We have carried religion across the seas to get to this country and fought like heck for it. I don't think that we're ready to loose it now! We have fought wars in the name of God and country and the "South" is still aiming towards that goal. Unfortuantley, some of our countrymen have forgotten what we are all aiming for, God and country.

"Hard work is needed in order to attain success and power."

You don't always get to choose what you witness in life. We are all here in this great country and should be striving for the same goals. If we have confidence we will persist in the face of challenges and ultimately overcome them. So, maximize your gains and minimize your losses. Enjoy the fruits of your labor and the sense of satisfaction that can be found through effort. Stand by your God, country and family. This my friends, is how you will find your way toward happiness!

"There is material gain and reward that is achieved through hard work and effort."

Chapter Eighteen

"It seems like I have been chasing my own tail all of my life."

We're all detectives in the mystery that we call life. Searching for clues to find out what we are all doing here. Trying to understand ourselves and the people that we care about.

Sometimes I feel good and free and then at other times I feel bad and I feel trapped. So, I scream at the moon! I know, I'm human. So are you. We laugh and we cry. That's life.

Someone once said; "If you are to absorbed with the trees in the forest, you may never find your way out of that forest."

You may be offered conventional wisdom, and you can politely ignore it or you can accept it. All you have to do is try and be a little better than you were yesterday in some way or another.

Take advantage of your expanding intellectual abilities. Have self-worth. It strengthens when you make decisions for your own best interest. Create a good foundation for your own personal life. The path that you didn't take will be a source of wonder. Perhaps you'll never know that version.

It is important to find new ways to do things, especially if the old ways have become rigid and imprisoning. The things that need to be examined and changed may come from society rather than from within us. We often live our lives as we have been taught to. Never examining closely whether our lifestyles really suits us. We simply carry on along the path that has been mapped out for us since childhood.

I say, challenge that complacency and, although we might decide ultimately not to change. The important thing is that we continually consider and evaluate new visions and possibilities. But, always remember the important things in life, the things that you were taught in your Grandma's kitchen.

Sometimes you should embrace your fears in life for it can heighten your perception and can help you to correct your course if need be. Be a little rebellious. A little bit of badness goes along way. It's easy to choose the good and the right thing to do once you've exhausted all other options. External incentives may temporarily work to keep you moving forward, but ultimately the only reliable motivation is the one that comes from within you. "I'm no daisey!"

"Admitting where the hurt is doesn't make you weak it only makes you stronger."

Try and have trust in the people that you come across. Without trust or a willingness to take a risk, no gains can be made. Fear is a great inhibitor to healthy growth.

And if you are in a period of difficulty then it must be endured with a degree of stoicism and fortitude, and that, although things may be uncomfortable, is the best way through it all. Do it with pride and self-respect.

"The time is ripe for change and the challenge must be met."

Expierence may be the best teacher in life, but her methods are not for the faint of heart. And always remember that laughter makes your health better and your life longer. So, try and laugh as much as you possibly can through it all.

"Let joy radiate out of you."

Heartache and difficulty is an unavoidable aspect of everyday life. The most important thing is to understand how to manage that pain. The fact that there is light behind the broken heart suggest that joy and sorrow are partners which can't be separated.

Facing and embracing the sorrow is the only way to get through bad times. Once the sorrow is properly mourned only then can it be possible to move on.

There is a feeling of 'the calm before the storm'. Nothing is actually wrong yet, but there seems to be mounting tension. Call it a woman's intuition.

In this world I predict a radical change is imminent. Something embryonic or not fully formed. There is a sense that, although the outlook might not be immediatley favorable, there may be a pleasant surprise in that something initially unpromising turns out to be quite positive after all.

"It's life that we deal in, the good and the bad. It's how we face it that matters."

Our goal in this life should be a move away from trying times and towards a period of peace and calm. Changing our enviroment or attitude from negative to positive can make a big difference. That which can release tension and strain giving way to a more peaceful phase of life.

The levels of energy and enthusiasm are still positive. Be realistic so that you do not over-inflate achievements nor over-rate the time they'll take to accomplish. And remember, Rome wasn't built in a day!

"The dawn is breaking in the horizon which suggest new life and light."

We are all like a sponge. Everything that we have absorbed in life we have to take it all in. (Wrap our head around it.) I, taking in everything that I learned from my Grandma's kitchen, Mom's kitchen and my own kitchen. The ingredients of life.

Y'all have a good life and may we all meet in the sweet by and by.

And y'all thought that this was just a cookbook.

"Life is a recipe, so get all of the ingredients!"

The End

Dedication:

This book is dedicated to my Granddaughter, Quinn Ann Marie Walsh who did not make it into this world. I truly believe that my relatives who have already passed over are looking after that little girl until we pass over. And when I pass over to the Great Beyond and I meet her for the first time, she'll know me as, "Nanna" and I'll know her as my Granddaughter, Quinn.

I also, want to dedicate this book to my Grandson, Brycen Kenneth and my Granddaughters, Emma Raylee and Olive Kinber because they are so cute and I want to teach them everything that I can from my kitchen.

Love, Nanna

Artwork by: Nancy Inman

LAST WILL AND TESTAMENT OF ABEDNEGO INMAN

In the presence of thes witnes present I acknoleg this my last will and testament. This land I now live on I give to my three suns Shedrach Inman, Benjamin Inman and John Inman at my wifes decease.

My thre dayters Annes Cowan, Polly Bair and Peggy Harriet Wood the remaind of my estat after my lawfiil detes is payd. I do not alow enything to be desttrebuted in during my wifes netuel lifetime but what I leeve sole executors of this my last will and desire it to be recevd the sem. I do not alou the land to be sold or devded into eny smauler porcels but the executors to do what tha think is rite and gusth the entry includ as land. Witness my hand this twevth day May One thousand eight hundred and thirty.

witnes s/Bed Inman
Nicholas Bragg

Mary her X mark Bragg

Archband T. McSpadden

State of Tennessee

Jefferson County March Sessions 1831

Bio

Nancy Inman grew up in Davy Crockett's Neck of the Woods in the South. She describes this part of God's country and some of the people who fought to live there. She also teaches you how to speak and understand "Southern".

Printed in the United States
By Bookmasters